P9-DVE-574

THE ART OF
HOME
CONVERSION

THE ART OF
HOME
CONVERSION

TRANSFORMING UNCOMMON PROPERTIES
INTO STYLISH HOMES

LORRIE MACK

SEVEN
·DIALS·

Editor: ISOBEL HOLLAND
Art Editor: LISA TAI
Picture Research: LORRIE MACK
Production: SUSAN BROWN AND
CHERYL COOPER

Special photography was done by
Shona Wood and coordinated by
Lorrie Mack

Frontispiece: Lodged on top of a
riverside warehouse, this sturdy brick
water tower has become a fantasy
dwelling with its own sky-level terrace
carved out of the original roof-top
storage tank. (See page 54.)

First published in the United Kingdom in 1993 by Cassell

This paperback edition first published in 1999 by
Seven Dials, Cassell & Company
The Orion Publishing Group
Wellington House, 125 Strand
London, WC2R 0BB

Text copyright © Lorrie Mack, 1993

All rights reserved. No part of this publication may be
reproduced in any material form (including photocopying
or storing it in any medium by electronic means and whether
or not transiently or incidentally to some other use of this
publication) without the written permission of the copyright
owner, except in accordance with the provisions of the
Copyright, Designs and Patents Act 1988 or under the terms
of a licence issued by the Copyright Licensing Agency, 90
Tottenham Court Road, London W1P 9HE. Applications
for the copyright owner's written permission to reproduce
any part of this publication should be addressed to the
publisher.

Distributed in the United States of America by
Sterling Publishing Co., Inc.
387 Park Avenue South,
New York, NY 10016-8810

A CIP catalogue record for this book is available
from the British Library

ISBN 1 84188 023 X

Printed in Hong Kong

Special Photography by Shona Wood,
coordinated by Lorrie Mack

To Richard Williams and Charles Middleton-Smith, who are
responsible for the conception and birth of this book respectively.

AUTHOR'S ACKNOWLEDGEMENTS
First, I want to thank all the owners of the homes featured
here, who were unfailingly generous and enthusiastic in sharing
their stories and their ideas with me, especially Anne Bickford-
Smith and Tony Tooth, Elizabeth Browning Jackson and Peter
Allen, Doug Patterson and Joanna Buxton, Lisa and Mark
Roper, David and Antonia von Soode, David Walker, and
Brian Withnell and Stuart Harling, who suffered the enormous
disruption and unimaginable intrusion of our photography
with grace and forbearance.
I am also grateful to Shona Wood, for the great skill and care
that went in to all her work; to Isobel Holland, for making the
editorial process not only straightforward and efficient, but also
unusually enjoyable; and to Lisa Tai who, as well as being a
pleasure to work with, managed to design exactly the book I
carried in my imagination for so long.
Sincere thanks are also due to the individuals and agencies who
supplied their photographs readily and resourcefully, then bore
with me patiently through many delays; to my agent, Barbara
Levy, who has put a great deal of time, effort and interest into
this project; and to colleagues and friends like Gillian Prince,
Rachel Duffield, Peter Butler, Isabel Moore and Phil Seddon,
whose support has been invaluable.

NOTE
In the period of time between preparation and publication of
this book, it is perhaps inevitable that changes have taken
place, and that some of the personal circumstances described
have altered. L. M. 1993

PICTURE ACKNOWLEDGEMENTS
The publishers would like to thank the following for their kind
permission to reproduce the photographs in this book:

Michael Boys/Boys Syndication 38, 39, 40, 41, 72, 73, 74, 75,
90, 91, 92, 93, 94, 95, 114, 115, 116, 117, 138, 139, 140, 141,
148, 149, 150, 151; Jacobs Island Company plc (Developer)/
Pollard Thomas Edwards & Associates (Architect) 16; Ken
Kirkwood 32, 33, 34, 35, 36, 37, 142, 143, 144, 146, 147; Ianthe
Ruthven 133, 134, 135, 136, 137; Fritz von der Schulenberg
2–3, 17, 18, 19, 48, 49, 50, 51, 52, 53, 54, 55, 56, 57, 58, 59, 60,
61, 62, 63, 64, 65, 66, 67 68, 69, 70, 71, 118, 119, 120, 121, 123;
Bill Stites 86, 87, 88, 89; Jessica Strang 132; Ron Sutherland 26,
27, 28, 29, 30; 31; Spike Powell/EWA 96, 97, 98, 99, 100, 101;
George Whiteside 42, 43, 44, 45, 46, 47; Shona Wood 7, 8, 9,
10, 11, 12, 13, 14, 15, 76, 77, 78, 79, 80, 81, 82, 83, 84, 85, 106,
107, 108, 109, 110, 111, 112, 113, 124, 125, 126, 127, 128, 129,
130, 131, 152, 153, 154, 155, 156, 157, 158, 159; World of
Interiors/Tom Leighton 102, 103, 104, 105, /James Mortimer
20, 21, 22, 23, 24, 25.

CONTENTS

INTRODUCTION

Those intrepid souls who choose to carve their home out of an
unlikely – and often derelict – property rather than settle for a
purpose-built one do so for a variety of reasons: some have a
yearning for vast expanses of open space, or simply want the
opportunity to organize their space to suit their own needs; others
are fuelled by a romantic zeal to rescue a neglected structure that
would otherwise fall into ruin; while for many more the main
priority is a domestic environment that is personal,
unconventional and unique.

Whatever their motivation, what all these architectural
adventurers seem to share is a powerful, emotional involvement
with their surroundings, a sympathetic feeling for the spirit of
their chosen building as well as its fabric, and – even at first sight –
an ability to look beyond a lack of plaster, plumbing and
electricity, and imagine it in every detail of its finished state.
Alongside this creative vision, they also have the indomitable
strength, incredible persistence and unshakeable determination
necessary to keep hold of their dream in the face of the endless
string of problems and delays, administrative as well as structural,
that a project of this kind often entails.

The twenty-five interiors illustrated in this book have all been
conceived by people with just these qualities, and their
resourcefulness and creativity has produced not only a wide range
of ingenious solutions to every kind of furnishing problem, but
also a wealth of inspirational decorating ideas that can completely
transform homes of every size and style.

A PICTURE PALACE

HAY LOFT

IN ORDER TO HOUSE HIS LARGE PIECES OF FURNITURE AND IMMENSE
COLLECTION OF PAINTINGS AND DRAWINGS, AN IMAGINATIVE
GALLERY OWNER TRADED A TRADITIONAL TOWN HOUSE FOR A VERY
UNUSUAL MEWS PROPERTY

As a former estate agent, David von Soode knew instantly that the
spacious mews property he had gone to view was unique. Space
had been his first consideration in looking for a new house, since he
needed somewhere big enough to accommodate himself, his wife
Antonia and their two children, plus the large collection of pictures
and furniture he inherited when his family estate was sold. A
traditional town house wasn't the answer though, since many of
these have endless storeys, and he was not prepared to negotiate
more than one flight of stairs. As well as generously sized rooms on
no more than two floors however, he wanted somewhere to live
that was a little bit different, and the former hay loft he'd heard
about through a friend fulfilled his requirements perfectly.

When he took it on, the conversion work had already been done,
but only just: the staircase was rudimentary, there were no
architectural features to speak of, and any kind of real style was
lacking altogether. Happily, style is something that David, an art
gallery owner who deals in mainly eighteenth- and nineteenth-
century paintings and drawings, possesses in vast quantities. His
previous house had been decorated in a traditional, chintzy manner, but he wanted a more dramatic treatment for this one and he
flirted, very briefly, with the kind of stark, minimalist look that

RIGHT: THE LIVING ROOM'S CAVERNOUS PROPORTIONS COULD HAVE BEEN
overpowering, yet its atmosphere is unusually warm and intimate. To achieve
this, the same softly glowing shade was chosen for walls, pitched ceiling and
beams – a pale honey hue that alters subtly with the light. Coir matting of the
same tone completes an unbroken sweep of background colour.

LEFT: LEADING UP TO
the main rooms, the hall
and staircase are hung
with eighteenth- and
nineteenth-century
pictures. The small
frames contain a
collection of 'fat people'
images, an affectionate
reference to David's
own imposing
proportions, while the
large portrait, by Sir
John Collier PRA, is of
his great-grandmother.
Since the wallpaper he
wanted wasn't available
in a suitable colour,
David had this one
printed to order.

many would think lent itself naturally to lofty, beamed rooms and
pitched ceilings. This aberration soon passed, and he realized that
both he and his wife valued comfort too highly to be happy in such
an environment, which in any case could never assimilate their
family treasures.

Having made the decision to let his possessions dictate the
character of the house, David began to cast around for ideas and
influences, certain only that he wanted the house to have a chunky,
masculine, vaguely William IV feeling. Blessed with a circle of
friends that includes many decorators and antique dealers, he was
not lacking for suggestions, but in the end his inspiration came
from two main sources, both well-known interior designers: the
late Geoffrey Bennison and David Mlinaric. In Bennison's rooms,
David found a sympathetic emphasis on warmth and comfort, a
love of opulently layered patterns and textures, and a taste for
books, flowers and exquisite objects in profusion. From Mlinaric's
work, he borrowed not only the concept of basically plain walls,
but also their subtle, specially mixed colours, as well as the choice of
simple coir (coconut fibre) floor covering, fitted wall to wall, that
makes a perfect background for his oriental rugs. The idioms of
these two masters work particularly well together in David's view:
he has little use for fussy decorating detail since, for him, a home's

RIGHT: THE STUDY END
of the living room has
large double doors that
open on to the dining
area at the top of the
stairs. Here, an entire
wall is covered with
custom-made bookcases
which, like all the
woodwork in the room,
have been given a dark
green eggshell finish. On
the easel is a another
ancestral portrait, this
one by Daniel Gardner;
the floor-standing
watercolour, by Serena
Vivian-Neal, is a mirror
view of the corner of the
room that faces it.

contents are of far greater importance than the shell around them. In addition, the design ethos of abundant, rich furnishings set against an unadorned background was ideal for someone who, although lucky enough to have inherited beautiful things, was not able to draw on unlimited funds to purchase elaborate wallpapers, carpets and window coverings as well.

In fact, David and Antonia re-used as many items as possible from their previous house, ruthlessly chopping down curtains where necessary in order to free as much of their budget as possible for semi-structural elements like the intricately constructed book-cases that take up a whole wall in the living room, and the imposing staircase leading up to the main rooms from the ground floor hall and entrance below – the only places where architectural details like cornices, mouldings and dado rails were added. Similarly, the stairs' original, somewhat spindly, balusters were replaced with thick, curved ones much more in keeping with the scale and the atmosphere of the building. All these things were designed by architect Robin Salmon in collaboration with his exacting client, and made by a craftsman-joiner to their specifications.

As successful as such alterations have been, they constitute only minor details that set off, exactly as David intended, the stunning

ABOVE: A RICHLY UPHOLSTERED CHAIR WITH MATCHING FRINGE (ONE OF A PAIR) and two pretty needle-point stools are typical of the antique textiles that David searches out enthusiastically; the tartan handle on the magnifying glass hints at another collection.

LEFT: DOMINATING THE ROOM IS AN UNUSUAL KILKENNY MARBLE FIREPLACE that was designed specially for it, while a huge oriental carpet (bought at auction) defines the main seating area. On every sofa and chair, exquisite tapestry or patchwork cushions are displayed singly, or in inviting piles.

furniture and accessories that absorb so much of his interest and affection. Obviously the most recent in a long line of inveterate accumulators, David has developed several collecting themes of his own, such as the textiles – precious rugs and tapestries, quilts, and fragments of soft, faded chintz – that he finds at country house sales, auctions, flea markets and junk shops. An assortment of tartanware articles, from small boxes and books to penknives and spectacle cases, bears his unmistakable stamp as well, along with the countless china pug dogs that guard the family photographs and mementoes. Not surprisingly though, the collection that stands out most dramatically is of pictures; wherever you look, oils, watercolours and charcoal sketches, portraits, landscapes and still life studies are grouped on the walls, standing on the floor, or stacked up on desks and tables, revealing not only David von Soode's profession, but also one of his abiding passions.

Although meticulously created in the not-too-distant past, these rooms don't seem at all contrived: somehow they feel as if they've always been there, developing and changing organically with time. This impression is not altogether misleading however, since David, never completely satisfied, is full of plans for buying new things and moving old ones around. Standing at the doorway of a room that few would argue is an object lesson in style and elegance, he remarks ingenuously, 'But the pictures don't quite work – no, it's not right, not really finished yet'.

Right: ILLUMINATED by one of the hay loft's several skylights, David's corner of the dressing room has been meticulously planned around his wardrobe; facing the Regency chair and peeping out from behind the chest of drawers, for example, are serried ranks of highly polished shoes. To the left, just visible in the mirror, are the shelves and rails that meet Antonia's storage needs.

Right: THE BEDROOM has a strong country-house feeling that is reinforced by the massive Victorian linen press, the chintz curtains with their gathered pelmets, and the softly colour-washed walls, which also help to minimize the irregular angle of the ceiling. This room contains only twentieth-century pictures, a relatively small collection that David wants to extend. The still life over the dressing table is by Sir William Nicholson.

SMALL-SPACE CRAFTS

GRAIN WAREHOUSE

METICULOUS PLANNING, A DESIGNER'S EYE FOR DETAIL AND THE
WORK OF MANY HANDS MADE IT POSSIBLE FOR A SMALL INDUSTRIAL
SPACE TO BECOME AN EFFICIENT, STYLISH STUDIO APARTMENT

People who live in warehouses normally do so to gain space; they
wax lyrical about huge, lofty rooms that liberate them from the
restrictions of a purpose-built dwelling. When Wendy Booth and
Leslie Howell took on their single 6 × 9m (20 × 30ft) room in a
riverside grain warehouse however, it was because they wanted to
get away from living on such an overpoweringly large scale. Some
years earlier, they had moved into their first commercial building,
which had typically vast rooms, but the novelty soon wore off.
Although they still liked the idea of a warehouse, they longed for a
smaller-scale home, one they could finish with exquisite design
details and fill with beautiful objects – almost like a miniature
museum with a warm, cosy atmosphere.

First though, they had to decide on a floor plan. While they were
quite happy to live, sleep and eat in one open area, they needed to
carve out space for the bathroom, and local fire regulations insisted
on a separate entrance lobby. In addition, they wanted a generous,
closed-off corner for dressing and storage. All these requirements
were met by installing an angled partition wall in an ingenious M-
shape against one end of the room, thus forming three small
triangular chambers (the storage space and bathroom flank the
lobby), and establishing a geometric theme that was later carried
through much of the flat's design.

Right: SOUGHT FOR AND DESIGNED AS A SHOWPLACE FOR ARTS AND CRAFTS
furniture, the flat is dominated by a sturdy oak sofa reproduced from an 1890s
design by Gustav Stickley, originator of 'Craftsman' style, the American version
of Arts and Crafts. Dating from the same period are the two Liberty 'Thebes'
stools at either end.

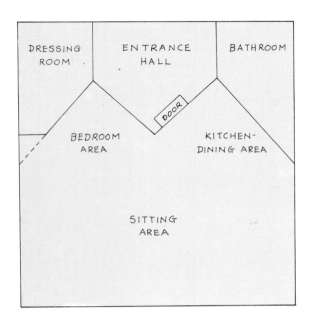

B̲ELOW: ENCLOSED ON TWO SIDES BY THE FLAT'S only partition wall (see diagram), the bed is covered with a silken cloth from Africa, woven for an Ashanti chief. Above it are triangular shelves and small windows that give on to the dressing area beyond; in front is an Art Deco table by Ambrose Heal. The cast iron columns and timber ceiling are part of the original Victorian fabric of the building.

The external brick wall was left alone, while the internal, plaster ones were washed with palest turquoise. Ideally, Wendy and Leslie would have liked a wooden floor, but hard surfaces create noise problems, so they chose instead two layers of cork: one insulating layer on the existing boards, then honey-coloured tiles on top, each one tinted a slightly different shade using artists' pigments like sienna and ochre. Joining floor to walls is a simple timber skirting embellished with a delicate, carved diamond pattern, which, like much of the flat's hand-crafted detailing, was the work of one of an astoundingly large assortment of talented friends. This motif is echoed on the bevelled lighting pelmet that runs across the room, concealing a row of tiny bulbs for subtle, indirect illumination, but here the shape is cut right out of the wood so the light can shine through. In some places, bits of blue and turquoise glass have been inserted to vary the effect. Direct, functional lighting comes from strategically placed anglepoise lamps while, at night, clusters of white candles flatter the room and its occupants.

Where possible, windows were left free of coverings; two are hung with inexpensive blue plastic blinds, and these provide a splash of really brilliant colour in a basically brick-and-wood landscape. When the sun is blinding, it is simply blocked out with one of the folding oak screens the couple use to define separate activity areas. The screens, like most of the rugs and items of furniture, are moved around constantly to create a shifting series of rooms within rooms. The kitchen units though, are permanently fixed, as is the bed, whose built-in base conceals a capacious storage compartment, accessible from both the main room and the dressing/storage cubicle on the other side of the adjacent wall.

The warm, natural textures and colours of the flat's fittings were chosen to set off the Howells' superb collection of late nineteenth-century Arts and Crafts furniture, most of it made from English oak. The style is one that fascinates Leslie, mainly because it represents the first attempt by cabinet-makers using traditional techniques and materials, to experiment with shapes that were completely new, and at odds with everything around them. Stroking one of his spare, linear dining chairs affectionately, he remarks, 'Isn't it incredible that this was once used by an Edwardian lady with a heaving bosom and a large bustle'.

When you consider how perfectly these hundred-year-old pieces suit a room – and a way of life – that is quintessentially modern, you can only agree with him.

R̲IGHT: BEHIND A LIBERTY DINING SET, OAK KITCHEN UNITS DISPLAY THE FLAT'S diamond motif in several ways; set in as mosaic tiles, cut out of the wood, and applied to the control panels – even the drawers have diamond-shaped holes instead of handles.

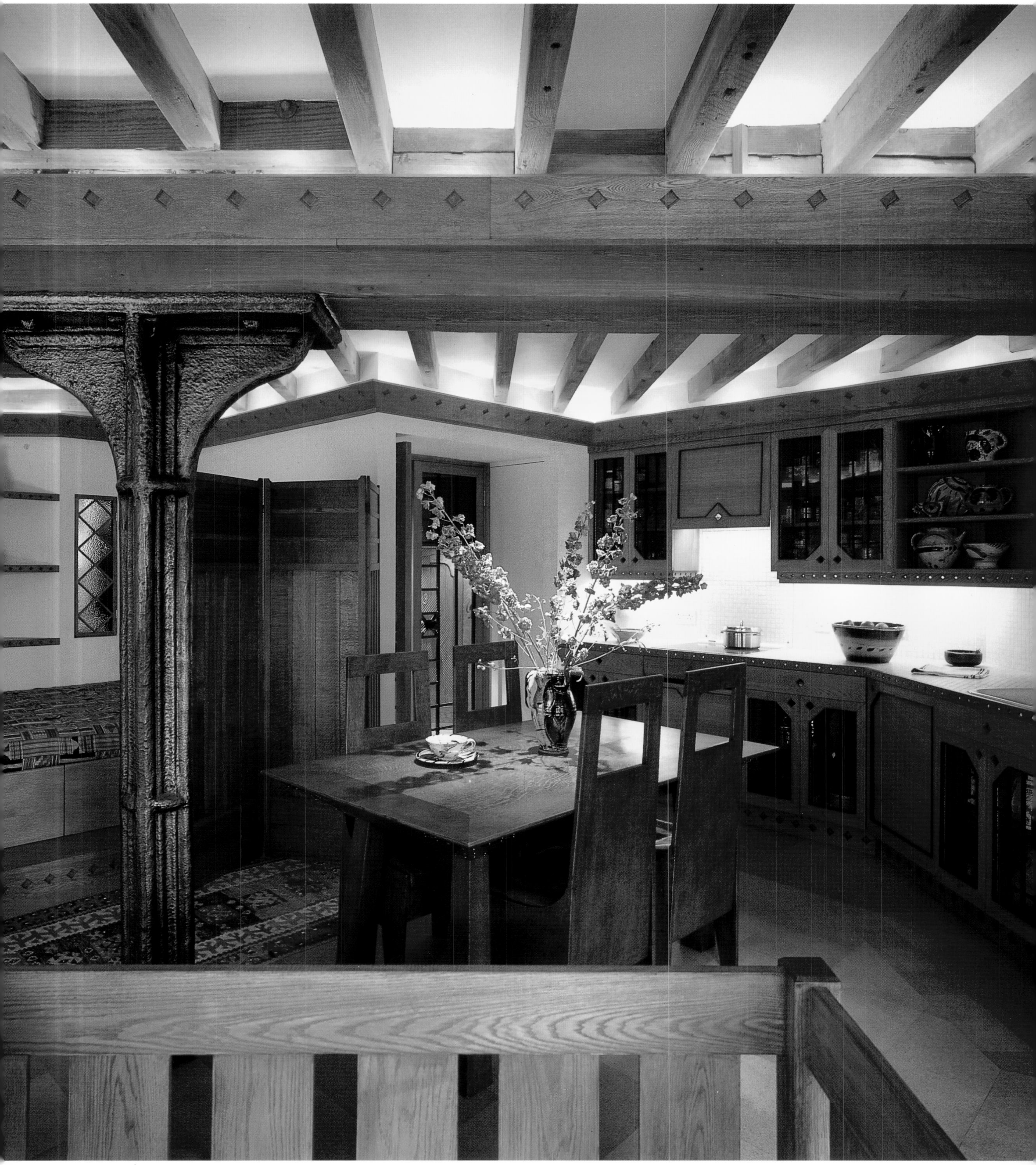

A BRUSH WITH TIME

COACH HOUSE

WHEN A GEORGIAN 'GARAGE' IS EMBELLISHED WITH INGENIOUS PAINT TECHNIQUES AND FILLED WITH EXOTIC ARTS AND CRAFTS FROM AFRICA, THE EFFECT IS RARELY CONVENTIONAL AND OFTEN INSPIRING

Although Mr and Mrs Gordon Wilson live in a beautiful coach house, and their previous dwelling was carved out of three crumbling barns, they profess to having no special interest in unusual properties. 'The most important thing about any potential home is its atmosphere', says Mrs Wilson. The instant she saw Pelham Cottage, she knew it was perfect for her, for a well-loved collection of early oak furniture and intricate textiles, and for the exotic artefacts she and her husband acquired during their years in West Africa, where he worked for a large trading company.

As far as Mrs Wilson is concerned however, *finding* a building with the right atmosphere is only the beginning. 'Every detail of decoration and furnishing should be there for a reason, from the approach to the property, through the garden, into every room inside.' Visitors can see evidence of this meticulousness as soon as they pass through the gate, which was custom made in an unusual arched shape to echo the pretty windows in the front of the house.

Although the building itself is Georgian, its owners felt instinctively that it could be coaxed back slightly further in time to complement their furniture. In fact, it is built on the site of an even earlier structure than they had in mind, a tenth-century priory, and one of the original stone walls still adjoins the house, concealing a modern extension. In order to reinforce the cool, formal feeling they sensed was right, Mrs Wilson gave the garden, originally of

RIGHT: THE DINING ROOM'S GENTLE CREAM AND TERRACOTTA HUES OFFER A perfect backdrop for the striking Abuja pottery that Mr and Mrs Wilson brought back from Nigeria. Above an enormous Elizabethan trunk is a picture by their daughter Althea that demonstrates her versatility with a paintbrush.

LEFT: ALTHEA'S
illusory blocks of stone
appear again in Pelham's
hallway which, like the
rest of the house, has
polished wooden floors
covered with beautiful
rugs and carpets – this
one is Persian. On top of
the chest is an early
English bowl, while at
the doorway, a pair of
Nigerian spears and a
swordfish tooth stand
guard.

the cheerful, tumbling, cottage variety, an almost Elizabethan look, its open spaces defined by straight rows of yew. Even the small back courtyard where the rubbish bins are kept is walled and floored with brick, and contains large, traditionally ball-shaped box trees in terracotta pots.

More than any other feature though, Pelham's massive stone walls establish its period atmosphere, yet these – apart from the original priory wall – are not so much the legacy of the ages as the inspired brushwork of the Wilsons' daughter Althea, who disguised the original, rather boring, rendering with a masterly *trompe l'oeil* treatment.

Inside, Althea's painterly skills (which are more usually employed on canvas than on concrete or plaster) were invaluable, since all the rooms, although appealingly high, are rather small. To give an impression of greater space (and to provide an appropriate setting for her pictures and furniture), Mrs Wilson wanted to keep the walls plain, yet she dislikes the dull, flat look that solid colours often give. Happily, Althea was able to create the desired impression of depth and texture without resorting to fussy patterns by drawing on her repertoire of paint techniques, from the baronial mock-stonework in the hall to the soft, subtle wash in the bedrooms, a look she describes as 'battered French'. As well as

BELOW: PELHAM'S
Georgian past has been
respected in the design
of the kitchen; all the
cupboard doors (one of
which conceals the
refrigerator) are old
shutters found at an
architectural salvage
company. Beyond the
fruit-wood table and oak
chairs (also Georgian), a
painted drum sits by the
back door, ready to
serve as an occasional
table inside or out. One
of Mrs Wilson's
favourite pieces is a set
of small pine drawers
that was originally a
chemist shop fitting;
now it holds cutlery and
utensils.

LEFT: THIS SIMPLE, BLUE bedroom is dominated by an embroidered coverlet worked by Althea to blend in with a scheme reminiscent of Africa, where indigo dye is a main source of colour. In order to shut out the sun without covering the radiators, Mrs Wilson designed an ingenious steel curtain rail which, like those throughout the house, was made up by the local blacksmith. Shaped like a flattened C lying on its front, this holds long, fixed, dress curtains at each side of the window, plus shorter ones behind that draw across when necessary.

solving a knotty design problem, these finishes are used to make intrusive modern features like radiators and pipes almost invisible, an important advantage in modestly sized rooms that can easily look cluttered. Another small-space tactic that Mrs Wilson has taken full advantage of is the use of mirrors: all over the house, large and small, plain and ornate examples make every area look bigger, as well as adding light and sparkle.

Interestingly, Pelham is full of light, despite having relatively small windows, and this is probably due to its ideal situation at the top of a hill. To admit as much sun as possible, to make the most of the spectacular views, and to show off the beautiful shape of these windows, Mrs Wilson has left them completely unadorned, or hung only the simplest possible curtains or blinds. Night-time illumination comes mainly from an assortment of church candlesticks, either filled with candles as intended or converted for electricity. These unusual candlesticks are only one of several collections among Pelham's treasures, many of which were gathered during the couple's time in Nigeria.

Their African sojourn has left them with much more than beautiful objects however; it is also responsible for the way they feel about their home. In a strange land, this had to provide an emotional and cultural, as well as a practical, focus in their lives. Possessions were particularly precious because they had to move house frequently, and surrounding themselves with familiar things was the quickest way to create a personal environment. Even though many years have passed, and the Wilsons are now settled back in the land of their birth, the dependent relationship they established with their habitat then is still a very strong one.

RIGHT: MRS WILSON'S textile collection, gathered together from old family pieces plus interesting 'bits' discovered in antique shops and sale rooms, is one of the drawing room's prettiest features, and its flowery theme is picked up by the bowls and jugs full of blooms that appear on every available surface. Against the wall is a William and Mary oyster inlay cabinet on a stand strung with pear wood.

SEA CHANGES

FISH STORE

THE TRANSFORMATION OF A CRUDE FISHERMEN'S STORAGE SHACK
INTO A SOPHISTICATED SEASIDE HOUSE HAS TAKEN AS ITS DECORATING
THEME THE NATURAL ELEMENTS AROUND IT: SAND, WATER, SKY AND
ASTONISHINGLY CLEAR LIGHT

The dramatic and beautiful beach house that photographer Ron
Sutherland and his wife Carolyn have worked so hard to create
started life as a granite wall. First constructed at the beginning of the
nineteenth century to keep sand out of the crescent-shaped
harbour, it later provided shelter for local animals, then served as
the base of a rough structure where fishing nets or sails were stored.
By the 1930s, it had been turned into a studio for one of the many
artists that were – and still are – drawn to this part of the country by
the outstandingly clear light.

A frequent visitor to the area as a child, Ron had always wanted
to make a home there. When, almost by chance, he discovered that
this property had just come on to the market, he made an
immediate offer for it, despite the fact that its roof had long since
gone missing and it was filled with heaps of rubbish, nicely soaked
through by the rain. None of this mattered much to him though,
since the fabric of the building was much less important than its
breathtaking location on the white sandy beach. The prospect of
rehabilitation was a daunting one however, which is why it was still
derelict a year later when he became involved with Carolyn, an expatriate Australian journalist who immediately fell in love with the
bright blue skies, open spaces and stunning sea views that were so
like her Melbourne home.

Together with a friend, architect Max Benthall, they launched a
major assault on the studio, razing it almost back to the drains, then

RIGHT: THIS STRIKINGLY HOCKNEYESQUE IMAGE IS ACTUALLY A REFLECTION IN
the oven door of the window opposite and the sea and sky beyond. Below it, the
cupboard door's grid design repeats the pattern of the glazing bars, while the
white-painted housing cabinet helps to support the staircase that wraps around it.

slowly building it up again as time and money allowed. Leaving what was left of the roof and the wooden walls intact, they removed the inner skin of ruined plaster, and inserted a layer of insulation fibre before repairing or replacing the original structure. Initially planned as a cheap, essentials-only conversion, the job was undertaken in stages, and ended up costing about ten times what Ron and Carolyn had intended to spend. Even so, when they consider the result, they have to agree they would do it again.

On the elevation that faces the sea, which is in fact the back, Benthall had originally planned a balcony in addition to the enormous window running the full height of the house. Unfortunately, the local planning committee rejected the balcony, but the Sutherlands can give access to the sea breezes through one of the window's panels, which is actually a door: from this, a ladder leads down onto the beach. Despite the large expanse of glass, the window is perfectly safe, having been designed by a structural engineer to resist even a full-force gale.

The internal layout of the house is a simple, open plan one; the ground floor space houses the living area and kitchen, plus a small lean-to bathroom at the back, while above it is a large sunny room that serves both as sleeping quarters and Ron's studio. In terms of decoration, the couple felt strongly that no fussy details or unsympathetic colours should be allowed to interfere with the overpowering presence of the sea and the sky, and the constantly changing vistas these create. They also needed all the visual space they could achieve, since the building is not a large one. To meet all these needs, they painted the rough granite walls in a pale grey tone that does not differ greatly from the material's natural appearance. All the woodwork, including the tongue-and-groove panelling, is glossy white, which also reflects the maximum amount of light. The most dramatic decorative feature is the floor, a shimmering, brilliant blue surface that was covered with three coats of clear varnish to give it a finish so reflective that at first glance you could be mistaken for thinking the furniture is floating on top of a swimming pool.

To retain the calm, open feeling, only necessary furnishing items have been given house room, and these are either left in their natural state, or painted to blend in with the cool, watery scheme; Ron and Carolyn wanted it to look like a rustic hotel complex or a sort of seaside ranch. One of the wittiest touches is the huge squashy

RIGHT: WHEN WINTRY STORMS RAGE, THE WINDOW'S DOUBLE GLAZING AND robust construction provide plenty of insulation, but as soon as sunny days arrive, the door is left open to let in the salty air and allow the wall-hung ladder to be lowered on to the sandy beach below.

sofa, covered in boldly striped, modestly priced deck-chair canvas. In the kitchen, work surfaces are made from black Cornish slate, which not only has the crisp, graphic appearance required, but has also turned out to be hardwearing and exceptionally easy to look after.

Despite its cool atmosphere, the house is toasty warm even in the bitterest weather, thanks to the traditional cast-iron stove that dominates the main room, its large, industrial flue running straight up through the house like an efficient central heating radiator. The installation of this range was a source of great amusement to many local friends, who had only recently jettisoned theirs in an attempt to remove all traces of the indigenous style that has been such an inspiration to the Sutherlands.

They can easily live with the affectionate amusement of their neighbours though; after seven years, they both still feel a frisson of excitement every time they walk through the door. The only problems they experience these days are those they've created for themselves in the shape of a recently arrived baby girl: for her, they will probably need to build an extra bedroom on the top, and Carolyn has already insisted that one of the sorely needed cupboards must be sacrificed to make room for a washing machine. Despite this upheaval however, they would never think of leaving; in fact, Ron claims that every moment spent away from their seaside sanctuary is devoted to working out how quickly they can get back.

RIGHT: BESIDE THE window stands a matt black stove with a drunken bend in its flue that has no practical use whatsoever – it was a whim of Ron's that his builder was happy to indulge. The stove's base is comprised of three slabs of granite from a local quarry. In the kitchen, open shelves hold tableware and cooking equipment carefully chosen to carry through the seaside colour theme.

LEFT: THE BEDROOM IS illuminated by the endless expanse of glass that dominates the entire house, since it rises up through a well cut into the floor (just visible at lower left), then becomes a huge skylight. The pine furniture in this room offers the only contrast to the nautical hues used elsewhere.

MILL POWER

FLOUR MILL

A GROUP OF DERELICT BUILDINGS PROVIDED AN UNUSUAL HOME FOR TWO ANTIQUE DEALERS WITH A STRONG SENSE OF THE THEATRICAL AND AN IMPRESSIVE COLLECTION OF TEXTILES AND FURNISHINGS

Having combed the countryside for over six months to find a house that appealed to them, Brian Withnell and Stuart Harling were too discouraged to follow up a tiny classified advertisement for a 'mill with outbuildings'. From experience, they knew this type of property to be expensive, and they were unwilling to have their hopes raised, then dashed again. When the same ad reappeared several times however, they decided to investigate.

As soon as they saw it, they knew their spirits were under serious threat once more; it was a brilliantly sunny day, and the Victorian red brick mill with its pretty windows was surrounded by wild flowers. Nearby was a long barn made from the same material, its derelict condition partly disguised by the masses of tangled greenery clinging to its sides. In every direction, the views were like something out of a child's story book, with small farms and patchwork fields tucked among the gently curving hills. The property was soon to be sold at auction, and because it was too late by that time for them to enter an advance bid, they were particularly anxious not to miss their chance on the day of the sale. When they arrived at the venue, they were dismayed to note that three other people were taking an interest. Brian and Stuart were inexperienced in auction procedure, so when bidding started at the reserve price, Brian immediately shot up his hand and shouted out a higher figure. The complete silence that greeted his outburst made it clear that he was the only bidder, and the mill could have been theirs for the reserve price. They later discovered that their 'rivals' were local ladies, attending the auction only out of curiosity.

RIGHT: ON THE PINE-PANELLED LANDING, PAPERWORK IS DONE AT A GILLOW desk beside a window hung with early twentieth-century crewel-work. In front is a Victorian gothic stool, while shelves hold books, Parian ware figures and part of a large collection of deed boxes.

Attached to the main structure, where they intended to live, was a kiln house that had once contained a steam engine to provide power for milling the grain, and above this rose a 21m (70ft) brick chimney. (When the mill was in operation, this annexe was apparently also used for slaughtering animals and making glue from their hooves.) The roof that covered both buildings was half slate and half corrugated iron, but all the slates on the barn were still intact, so they were removed for use on the house; not surprisingly, the barn immediately collapsed. Later, Brian cleared away the rubble, and tidied up the ruin so it formed the walls for a series of garden 'rooms'.

The mill's front elevation was left exactly as they found it, each window replaced with an exact copy. The other walls had windows and doors added as necessary, but again, these were carefully matched to those already in place.

Inside were assorted pieces of broken-down equipment and endless piles of straw; to save money, they cleared all this away themselves on weekend visits. What they found underneath was essentially two open levels, with two small galleries above the lower one for storing sacks of grain. They were anxious to keep the space untouched, so one of these became a landing between the two

ABOVE: DESPITE ITS period feeling, the dining area is full of fakes: the repro chairs are in a style their owners have dubbed 'early Lion in Winter'; the chestnut table is supported by metal bars made to reinforce concrete; and the bleached oak cabinet was crafted in the 1930s. This room and the kitchen are both floored with terracotta tiles.

RIGHT: THE KITCHEN IS set off from the dining room by a brick peninsular unit. Supported by curly brackets, the pine wall cupboard holds a collection of jelly moulds.

ABOVE: THEIR BRICK structure left exposed, the mill's two chimney breasts contain efficient wood-burning stoves. Facing the one in the living room is an eccentrically high sofa in the Queen Anne style, covered in figured silk. Near the front door is a nineteenth-century Italian table made from walnut with barley-sugar twist legs and stretchers. The large gilt-framed picture is by Harold Dearden.

floors, but the other one had to be removed, since it was too low to allow the area under it to be used at all. The upper, wooden floor was completely rotten and had to be replaced, but the ground floor, which had been roughly concreted, provided a base for the damp-proof course. On top of this, over most of the floor area, they laid a new skin of smooth concrete, which was later stained, polished and scattered with rugs. The architect who drew up their plans wanted to raise the level of the floor at the kitchen end so they could see out of the windows during meals. At first, desperately short of money, his clients rejected the idea, but he was irritatingly adamant, and in the end, he won out. They, and their guests, have every reason to be grateful, since breakfasting around the sturdy refectory table while looking out over the surrounding uplands is one of the great joys of the house.

In the middle of the ground floor, supporting the beams, are two iron pillars that had also been used to steady the movement of the heavy machinery. To conceal and fireproof these, and to provide a channel for electrical cables, Brian and Stuart clad them ingeniously with half-cylindrical coping bricks. At one end of the house, they put in a chimney breast running its full height, plus two fireplaces, one on each floor. These were intended to heat the house completely, but it took only one freezing winter to reveal their inadequacy, and now a wood-burning stove has been installed, supplemented by electric storage heaters.

The building had power laid on but, despite its proximity to two houses, the authorities claimed there was no existing water, so a separate pipe would have to be laid from the mains supply some distance away. By sheer chance, one of the builders had worked in the mill as a boy and clearly remembered water being available; unwilling to be told otherwise, he searched the property until he found the stopcock, thus saving Brian and Stuart a huge, and completely wasted, expense.

When the structural work was completed, all the rooms were given a coat of soft white paint. Instead of curtains, old kelim rugs or faded tapestries cover the windows, often pulling to one side only. The simple poles from which they're hung are actually cheap lengths of brass tubing, while the 'finials' are cupboard knobs of the same material screwed into a plug of wood hammered in each end.

Brian and Stuart sell antiques, and their decorating style reflects this, both in the confidence and skill with which they've created a solid, masculine, country-house style, and in the rapid turnover of individual pieces; neither of them are quite sure, for example, how many dining tables they've gone through. Most of the furniture dates from the eighteenth or nineteenth centuries, and is crafted in walnut or oak (either dark or bleached), often with an unusual or even eccentric design. When it comes to smaller items, three major collections are very much in evidence: the first two, blue and white china from the Elkin Knight or Mason's Ironstone factories, and twentieth-century British painting, are there simply because of their visual appeal. The third collection though, of theatrical artefacts such as musical scores, costume designs, and model sets, has a much more practical origin – Brian worked for over twenty years as a stage hand at the Royal Opera House, Covent Garden, and Stuart is an operatic baritone who has performed with many leading companies.

The house is full of flowers from the large, informal garden, which was laid out on the principle that planting should be strictly controlled while looking as natural as possible. Here, old-fashioned blooms cling to the warm red brick walls or tumble unexpectedly over the ruined barn, and hidden corners are full of sweet-smelling lavender and sage.

Far away from urban crush and theatrical artifice, Brian and Stuart have managed to fulfil more of their original dreams than they ever thought possible.

ABOVE: THE MASTER BEDROOM IS DOMINATED BY solid oak furniture: a nineteenth-century coffer sits at the foot of the bed, while at its head is an eighteenth-century panel that was originally the front of a similar storage chest. Both the curtains and the coverlet are Victorian crewel-work – the latter bears the embroidered signature 'Sophia Harvey 1879'. Beside the bed, the plant-stand is an Art Nouveau design made entirely from ceramic (including the *trompe-l'oeil* inset stones), and the rug is an old Shiraz kelim.

TAKING STEPS

BALLET STUDIO

ONE ART FORM REPLACED ANOTHER WHEN A LARGE, LOFTY AND
BRILLIANTLY LIT DANCE STUDIO WAS REMODELLED BY AN
ENTHUSIASTIC YOUNG ARTIST INTO AN ALMOST PERFECT PLACE TO
LIVE AND WORK

Not content with finding a home that had once been something
else, painter Kate Shaw and her husband Brian MacGreevy ended
up in one that had *two* previous incarnations. Nestled in a tiny
mews behind a row of imposing mansions, the two-storey house
once accommodated a coach and several horses belonging to one of
the wealthy families who lived there; the top floor would have
provided space for hay, and perhaps a sleepy stable boy. Earlier this
century however, the clatter of hooves was exchanged for the
patter of pointe shoes when it was converted into a ballet school
with changing rooms and offices on the ground floor, and a studio
with the necessary sprung wooden floor upstairs.

In her single days, after a long search for 'something different',
Kate fell instantly in love with this property because it surprised and
delighted her on her initial visit; the entrance was unprepossessing,
the lower rooms were darkish and poky, and the stairs were rather
ordinary. Yet at the top of them she found an enormous sunny
room with a pitched ceiling, a big skylight, and the potential to
provide her with the perfect personal and professional
environment.

Although Kate was used to working with colour and space (her
paintings are mostly dreamlike vistas and impressions of exotic
landscapes), she felt in need of professional guidance when it came
to making use of this potential, so she consulted interior designer
Rachel Austin, a long-standing family friend. Eschewing the safe,

RIGHT: THE STUDIO'S SUNNY YELLOW WALLS WORK SURPRISINGLY WELL AS A
flattering surface against which to display pictures; the study of Christ on a
donkey that hangs over the shelves is by Kate's mother. In front of the sofa lies a
kelim rug woven in the happy colours that suit this room so well.

neutral scheme that many of her clients would have required, Rachel suggested strong, bright hues that Kate's trained eye felt perfectly comfortable with: daffodil yellow for the walls, deep rosy pink for the plain Roman blinds at the windows, and clear sky blue on the chunky sofa that was a gift from her mother. The rest of the room's furnishings pick up these main colours, whose intensity is relieved by the plain white floorboards and ceiling, and the subtly striped cream curtain that defines a sleeping area in the short arm of the studio's L shape.

The opposite corner from this is set aside for Kate's work, a large easel supporting the current project and a designer's plan chest coping with brushes, paints and chalks. Downstairs, the much smaller rooms house a pink kitchen and utility area, plus, on the same level, etching facilities that she sometimes hires out to friends and students.

The disparately sized rooms are linked though, by both brilliant colours and the wealth of idiosyncratic things – pictures, china, shells, books – that fill them, most of which have a sentimental association or an interesting history, since they were given as wedding presents, donated by family members, or gathered on holidays abroad.

The atmosphere Kate and Brian have created in their charming, quirky house is one of cheerful bustle and creativity, and this can't have changed much since the time when small girls danced their first steps there. These days however, the laughter of friends and music from the stereo replace childish giggles and the unmistakable tinkle of a ballet-class piano.

Right: DIVIDING THE living area from Kate's work space is a vast, deeply padded sofa covered in multi-coloured crewel-work fabric. A greater degree of privacy was required for the sleeping area though, so the couple chose filmy cream curtains that close off the area completely, yet still allow light to filter through.

Left: ACTING AS BOTH storage facility and bedside table, the inlaid chest of drawers was an antique shop find. A rush-seated ladder-back chair holds strings of beads and acts as a catch-all for clothes when necessary, while behind it, partially obscured, is a portrait of Kate.

WOOD NOTES
PLYWOOD WORKSHOP

AN UNCONVENTIONAL APPROACH TO SPACE AND AN INSPIRED MIX OF
MODERN CLASSIC FURNITURE WITH WITTY, INDIVIDUAL DESIGN
TOUCHES LIFT A CITY LOFT CONVERSION INTO A CLASS OF ITS OWN

If, as Sir Peter Ustinov observed, Toronto is what New York would be had it been designed by the Swiss, then architect Diane Bald's sleek loft conversion at the end of a downtown alleyway shares with its city many of the qualities that inspired the remark: efficient planning, a clean, modern character and a reassuring atmosphere of security and permanence.

This last feature, a particularly important one to Diane and her fashion-executive husband Michael Budman, is reinforced by their home's location in a vast, white, fortress-like brick structure whose existence is unsuspected even by those who regularly work or shop in one of the busy surrounding streets. The building was originally a plywood warehouse and marquetry workshop, and at first sight its ideal location (very central, yet near to their previous home and a much-loved local park), plus its enormous proportions, held such strong appeal for the couple that they took on the small amount of floor area that was originally for sale, then added further sections as they became available.

Once installed, they immediately removed all the unpleasant non-opening modern windows and fitted more sympathetic ones whose design resembles as closely as possible that of the standard factory originals. Next they ripped out the acres of plasterboard forming internal walls and covering every conceivable surface, an exercise that not only exposed the supporting structure of solid wooden beams and steel girders, but also left them with two vast

RIGHT: BEGINNING AS IT MEANS TO GO ON, DIANE BALD'S APARTMENT HAS AN entrance hall that is dominated by an unexpected mix of styles: a formal grand piano next to Fortuny's dramatic standard lamp. The Andrée Putman console table is another modern classic, while behind it is a typical business-like Bald touch – venetian blinds concealing the furnace.

LEFT: AN OPEN LIGHT well on the upper level is child-proofed with a sleek metal grid. This geometric theme is carried through in the totally Écart-furnished living room where an Eileen Gray rug sits in front of a sofa by Jean-Michel Frank, the brilliant French interior designer of the 1920s and 30s. Two huge windows with their uninterrupted expanses of glass are left free of any covering.

RIGHT: SET APART from the living room by its glowing oak floorboards, the kitchen area has brilliant white units topped with satin-finished sheets of stainless steel. Adding a hint of Deco style are the curved handles on the cupboards and drawers, which were picked up for only a few francs in a Paris hardware shop.

open floors. The functional ground level is made up of the entrance hall, TV and stereo room, laundry and utility space, Budman's dressing area and a playroom for their small son, while the upper, more sophisticated, tier has an almost entirely open-plan layout that contains the living room, dining room and kitchen, two bedrooms and a bathroom, separated, when necessary, by sliding *shoji* screens made from translucent glass panels supported by slender wooden frames, a sturdier version of the traditional Japanese model in delicate paper.

The stunning design scheme that Diane worked out for both floors is not bound by the conventions of any single period or country, but it is indelibly stamped with her distinct personal style. This style, she readily admits, has been strongly influenced by her association with the legendary French designer Andrée Putman, whose company, Écart International, is responsible for reproducing and marketing much of the famous modern classic furniture from the 1920s and 30s, including pieces by such luminaries as Le Corbusier and Eileen Gray. Diane first worked for Putman in Paris in the early 1980s, then later supervised some of her widely acclaimed work in the United States, including the St Laurent chain of stores, and the conversion by Studio 54's Steve Rubell and Ian Schrager of a seedy downtown rooming house into Morgan's, one of the most elegant and fashionable hotels in Manhattan. Fans of Putman's cool, chic look will recognize in Diane Bald's home characteristic elements such as the vast, uninterrupted internal space, the crisp black-and-white colour theme, and the confident

ABOVE: RAISED ON TO AN ILLUMINATED PLATFORM, the black-and-white tiled bathroom is pure Putman, inspired by her designs for Morgan's hotel in New York. There are no doors anywhere, even on the toilet recess; Diane maintains that the presence of a small child quickly dispels any inclination towards modesty.

RIGHT: ONE OF MICHAEL'S FAVOURITE OBJECTS IS this extraordinary clock, designed in 1935 and made entirely from Ford automobile components.

FAR RIGHT: THE LARGE DOUBLE BED AND LOW headboard-cum-display surface have been constructed as a single unit; cantilevered out from it are quarter-round glass shelves for bedside necessities. Further Gallic influence is evident in the pristine white bed-linen and the arrangement of square pillows supported by a fat bolster.

mix of old and new furniture with dramatic accessories chosen for their unusual shape or their surface texture, which is often shiny or even mirrored.

In order to cope with two busy adults and a small child however, all the furnishings had to be practical and hardwearing as well as attractive, and this requirement is satisfied by clever design choices such as the toddler-proof lacquer walls, the washable 50s-look Naugahyde (leatherette)-covered kitchen banquette seating that lifts up to provide extra storage, and the cheap, flexible linoleum covering the solid concrete at ground level. The witty and colourful cut-out motifs on this floor were more or less worked out as it was being laid – the tiler arrived a week earlier than expected, and rather than turn him away, Diane dropped everything and instantly produced a series of designs that ingeniously reflect individual areas of use: a rabbit-eared television and a set of musical notes in the TV and stereo room for example, and educational feet-and-metre graphics in the play area.

Miraculously, the entire conversion was completed in three months, a timespan made even more remarkable by the fact that it coincided with the last two months of Diane's pregnancy and her first few weeks of motherhood. No major changes had to be made after that and the only additional work was done two years later, when the couple added a roof-top terrace and the striking oak-and-metal spiral staircase that gives access to it. Undoubtedly, Diane Bald's professional training and experience contributed to the success of the project, but another major factor is clearly her down-to-earth attitude and healthy order of priorities; despite having created an interior that is both boldly innovative and superbly stylish, she sums up her feelings about it by saying simply, 'It's a very easy space to live in'.

PUTTING BACK THE DOCKS

TEA WHARF

THE RESCUE AND RENEWAL OF A CRUMBLING RIVERSIDE DEPOSITORY
WERE MADE POSSIBLE BY ONE WOMAN'S INDOMITABLE SPIRIT AND
REMARKABLE FLAIR FOR INTERIOR DECORATION

An enthusiastic journalist once called Rae Hoffenberg 'arguably the best architect alive today' – a flattering tribute, but an unexpected one in view of the fact that Mrs Hoffenberg has no formal training in the subject. Never one to avoid such contradictions, she tends to give forth a stream of invective at the excesses of many interior decorators, yet for over thirty years she has earned much of her living from this profession.

Born into a family of South African building developers, Rae spent many childhood hours with her father, pouring over plans, inspecting sites, and developing a fascination with architecture that was only one aspect of an obsessive visual awareness. Having taken a degree in fine art before her marriage, she drifted into doing schemes for her friends, then their friends, until she had her own business in Durban; as long ago as the 60s she was importing modern classic furniture by Mies van der Rohe and Breuer into South Africa – the first person to do so. Then, as now, she had little in common with others in the same line, as is evident from her view of them. When it comes to allocating a budget, for example, she is horrified at the idea of spending thousands on fashionable curtains and carpeting: for her, every home should be a powerful expression of its owners' personalities, so they would be much better advised, she feels, to invest in a piece of furniture or a picture they absolutely

RIGHT: THE LONG, WIDE ENTRANCE TO RAE HOFFENBERG'S DOMAIN HAS BEEN utilized to full effect; across from prints by Miró, Nolan, Appel and Pasmore, simple plank shelves accommodate many of her treasures: books on decorating and other applied arts, a collection of ink-wells from all over the world, and an assortment of old microscopes and magnifying glasses.

love, and one that can be taken with them when they move. She sees her role mainly as that of guide, helping clients to develop their own style and make the very best use of the space, and the furnishings, they already have.

When she arrived in London with her husband in the early 70s, they took on a large Georgian house in a pretty square. She couldn't be happy there though, since huge expanses of sky and light, which no amount of design expertise could reproduce, were vital to her. One of her favourite areas had always been the docklands, by the river, and she often went for pleasure drives there, among what she called the 'sleeping warehouses'. Most of these were owned by faceless, uncaring corporations, but on one of her excursions, she spotted an eighteenth-century Hudson Bay Company tea wharf that was up for auction. Having obtained the key, she opened the door and a flock of seagulls flew out from what Rae could only guess was their personal lavatory. On the far side of the cavernous space though, there was an opening onto the river through which the bales would have been unloaded. From this she could actually feel the waves splashing, and see the views of water and birds that Turner and Whistler had painted. The effect was overpowering: she made up her mind that she would live there and, with the backing of an enlightened financial institution, she bid for the property successfully. What she hadn't realized however, was that it had no planning permission for change of use from industrial to residential; she didn't even know such permission was necessary – she had expected simply to up tools and begin work. The main problem she faced was that there was no precedent – no one had ever been granted, or even applied to make, such a change in this area. Her struggle took three heartbreaking years of refusals, appeals, and deferments before a final, desperate appeal directly to the appropriate government department was successful.

Without pausing to draw breath, she immersed herself in the huge tasks of renovation and conversion; with extraordinary energy, she acted as architect, engineer and building foreman, hiring professionals only as draughtsmen and labourers. The 60cm (2ft) thick walls were robust, and the floor levels already established, but every other feature of the finished structure is a result of Rae's work. Because she had taken on this project purely out of love for the building and a commitment to making it her home, she

LEFT: HER LOVE OF NATURAL MATERIALS LED RAE TO ESCHEW PLASTER WALLS in favour of exposed brick ones. In the living area, seating takes the form of a daybed from colonial India and, on the right, a seventeenth-century English ratchet chair. Meals are served from an oak buffet of the same period, and eaten at a Queen Anne table surrounded by leather-backed chairs. A huge gilt-framed mirror hangs on the wall that forms the kitchen.

ABOVE: IN ADDITION TO BRICK, THE BATHROOM also features wood, marble and a wide expanse of glass in its design. The heated towel rail and pillar-cum-belt-rack indicate the practical side of the apartment's occupant, while exquisite collections of shells, scent bottles and storage containers reveal her aesthetic sensibilities.

RIGHT: RAE FEELS STRONGLY THAT THE KITCHEN should be an extension of the main living space, and she has decorated hers accordingly, with no intrusively white, shiny surfaces to be seen. She also likes cooking equipment to be displayed rather than hidden away, so the pale oak units have cupboards and drawers only underneath the tiled work surfaces – hanging racks and open shelves hold everything from salad bowls, pewter plates, copper pots and eighteenth-century glass to an impressive library of cookery books.

brought to this task a degree of perfectionism that no hungry developer could aspire to. Each beam and rafter, for example, was numbered, then removed, sandblasted, treated and replaced in its original position. One of the trickiest feats of engineering was enlarging the windows, yet keeping their distinctive, gently arched shape. Wherever possible, all materials were salvaged and re-used, and the scale and atmosphere of the building lovingly preserved. Slowly, in a space where most developers would have squeezed in ten or twelve poky flats, she carved out four, each one designed by her down to the last detail, and completely unique.

When the project was finished, she sold three of the flats and moved into the remaining one herself. Larger than many four-bedroom houses, it is ingeniously organized into what she calls 'internal suites' that flow into each other rather than being partitioned off with walls: even her bathroom is open plan so she can soap herself and chat to guests at the same time. A showcase for her design theories, the main rooms are full of natural colours and textures, with no curtains, and only the plainest cream carpet against which to display her oriental rugs; like many warehouse dwellers, she was prevented from leaving the floorboards bare by problems of sound insulation. Since part of Rae would be supremely happy living in a greenhouse, the main furnishing accessory is a huge and lush collection of plants – some the size of trees – whose foliage climbs up the rough brick walls and over the beams. The enormous rooms are filled with furniture and objects she has collected during her travels, or inherited from her family in South Africa: ironically, many items had been shipped out from England or France originally, only to be sent full circle back to Europe a generation later. The mix is an eclectic one: a French rococo table sits happily near a plain English oak chest, a testament to her innate sense of harmony and balance.

After the enormous success of this conversion, Rae went on to do several others, mainly out of fear that beautiful buildings would be ruined by unsympathetic treatment. Later, when the first hard-nosed estate agents came sniffing around, they brought potential backers to see her buildings, and her own flat, as a supreme example of what warehouse living had to offer. Because her work was done on a small scale however, and she isn't concerned with making huge profits or courting personal publicity, she has never received full credit for being the very first colonist of an area that is now undergoing the most intense, successful – and rapid – development in the history of the city. What she *has* done is identify and acquire her ideal location, and in it carve out the domestic environment of her dreams, an awesome accomplishment even for someone driven by the passion and perfectionism of Rae Hoffenberg.

DEVELOPING TRENDS I
WATER TOWER

AN INGENIOUS FLOOR PLAN AND A FANTASTIC DECORATING SCHEME
TURNED THE PRECARIOUS BRICK STRUCTURE PERCHED ON TOP OF A
DECAYING WAREHOUSE INTO A UNIQUE URBAN DWELLING

If one person can claim to have sparked off the wholesale revival of London's docklands, it is property developer Andrew Wadsworth. Although the loft culture had been fashionable in New York for several years before his arrival on the scene, and there were isolated pockets of it in the empty commercial buildings along the river Thames (like Rae Hoffenberg's tea wharf), the main surge of interest was inspired by his dramatic rescue and transformation of New Concordia wharf, a group of derelict grain warehouses.

Far from setting out to change the riverside landscape, Andrew initially went looking simply for a home that filled both his needs and those of his wife Julie Balmforth, a painter; he wanted to be near the water, while she had the rather more eccentric desire to colonize a building that had never been lived in before. The obvious answer was to find space in a docklands warehouse, and it was during one of their reconnaissance drives around the area that they came across the sorry structures that were to become the focus of both his personal and professional lives. Built in 1885, these were near collapse from age and neglect, and their demise was about to be hastened by a demolition contractor whose prominently displayed sign indicated a starting date only a few days away. The solid elegance they once had was still apparent though, and both Andrew and Julie knew they would respond magnificently to

RIGHT: FLANKING THE TORCH-BEARING EGYPTIAN LADY FRAMED BY ONE OF THE huge arched windows are four grand fluted columns. These are actually radiators, made by bending conventional panels into cylindrical shapes with the pipe side out, then painting them black, banding them with gold and setting them on square plinths. The pale hardwood floor is maple.

knowledgeable, sympathetic restoration. As soon as he could get to a phone, Andrew tracked down and harangued the owner who finally, at well past the eleventh hour, agreed to sell. With a devastating combination of chutzpah and sang-froid, Wadsworth had, at a stroke, risked his financial stability and his career on a building so decrepit that no surveyor would value it, and one that, in any case, he hadn't enough money to buy.

Buy it he did, however, with the help of a visionary merchant banker. Once that was accomplished, and plans were drawn up to turn it into an imaginative complex of offices, apartments, studios and showrooms, he and Julie needed to decide on a site for a home somewhere inside. As far as they were concerned, this had to be the large brick water tower at the top, from whose roof they could choose to gaze over the city skyline or the flowing river. Their decision was taken despite the less-than-inspiring vistas inside; since there were hardly any windows, all the couple could see was four open floors, grimy bricks and pigeon droppings.

At this point, they commissioned architect Piers Gough, who won't even take on clients unless they show a degree of respect for the original fabric and spirit of a building that matches his own. He drew up three schemes, all of which retained the original frame-work of four floors: two with low ceilings alternating with two that had lofty ones. The plan they finally chose was based around a series of linking staircases, which did not sit one above the other in the usual way, but travelled around the building, defining the spaces inside it.

On paper, the major alterations involved punching out six arched windows, installing the stairs, and constructing a gallery above the double-height top storey; in practice, two of the walls were in such appalling condition that they had to be completely demolished and rebuilt, a feat of engineering infinitely greater than the 'punching out' initially envisaged. Once the walls and windows were in place, Gough turned to the design of each floor.

His idea was to divide the two low ones into separate rooms, which would then be plastered and carpeted, so that very little visual evidence remained of the original structure. The higher storeys were to be left as close to their natural condition as possible, with large, open spaces and exposed surfaces like brick and wood.

At the base of the tower then, are two guest bedrooms plus bathroom. Above them is a single high chamber that serves as a billiard room-cum-library and occasional party venue; at one side,

TOP: IN THE BOTTOM-LEVEL BEDROOM, WALLS AND ceiling have been painted white to set off the Arts and Crafts furniture and accessories, all late nineteenth-century British. Of the two ceiling beams, one is real, the other faked to echo it.

ABOVE: NEXT DOOR, THE BEDROOM'S COLOUR scheme has been carried through in the choice of deep turquoise Spanish tiles for the walls, and bright blue paint for the traditional roll-top bath.

LEFT: UNDER THE KELIM, THE BILLIARD ROOM'S PINE FLOOR, LIKE ITS CEILING, IS original. To expose both of these, Gough had to put the required layers of fireproofing material below the floor of one low storey, and above the ceiling in the other, reducing their height even further.

a staircase leads to the next floor, and this is the level at which you enter the tower from the lift running up from the street. Just inside the front door, a wide, central stairway goes up through the other low level (where another bedroom and bathroom are sited) to the main storey, which houses the kitchen and dining room, plus a small sitting area. The gallery Gough fixed above this top floor (at a height determined by the position of the tower's only original windows) provides an intimate, cosily carpeted living area, reached by another flight of stairs that curves gently along one wall. Here, Gough realized one of his long-standing fantasies by installing a fireplace whose flue passes straight out through one of the windows.

The last staircase runs from this level up the outside of the tower to the roof terrace on top, which was originally a huge cast-iron water tank 1m (3ft) deep. It had to be as wide and shallow as this in order to distribute the weight of the enormous volume of water needed for milling grain, over a large enough area to support it.

ABOVE: THE ENTRANCE HALL AND STAIRS ARE MARBLE, THE HANDRAIL and detailing are mahogany, the chandelier is Venetian glass and the radiators and balusters have been gilded. At the door, is a Charles Rennie Mackintosh chair with its typically linear construction and exaggerated height.

RIGHT: BECAUSE HIS CLIENTS DIDN'T WANT A CONVENTIONAL KITCHEN, GOUGH housed the necessary equipment in an ersatz architectural ruin created entirely with paint effects; the 'marble' work surfaces are all made from Corian. Directly above is the galleried living area.

These external stairs not only provide access to the terrace without cutting into the metal sides, but also act as a fire escape.

The tower's fairly small dimensions, about 6 × 9m (20 × 30ft), together with its preponderance of staircases, gave it a slightly nautical feeling, and this led the Wadsworths and their architect to settle almost immediately on a decorative scheme that suggested a 1930s ocean liner. They all instinctively agreed on a watery colour palette of turquoise and eau de nil, plus a bold, bright blue that also linked up with the detailing on the building's exterior. Finding the furnishings to go inside however, did not have to be done in a hurry, since designing and rebuilding the tower took four years from start to finish. During this time Andrew and Julie lived in what he calls a 'sophisti-squat', in an undeveloped part of the warehouse below, so he could be near *The Harpy*, an Edwardian customs and excise pontoon moored nearby, from which he runs his business. Over this period, they were able to assemble a small collection of Arts and Crafts pieces, as well as several beautiful Art Deco and modern ones, and to search for exactly the right materials and accessories, not all of them rare or expensive; the simple white curtains hung throughout for example, are made from an incredibly cheap fabric called Bolton sheeting, which is normally used as the under cover on upholstered furniture.

Although it's often said that forming a client-architect relationship is a perfect way to end a friendship, there were an unusually small number of disagreements between them when it came to deciding what was right for the tower and for them. In fact, Gough found them to be ideal patrons, willing to see his ideas put into practice even when they felt unsure of the result; the fact that the three of them remained close friends when the job was finished is a testament to the success of the partnership.

Despite the brilliance of the finished scheme, however, the tower did not turn out to be a long-term home for Andrew and Julie; in the end, they found that being so very close to Andrew's business became increasingly like living over the shop – their private life ceased to be their own. In addition, they began to long for a slightly less theatrical domestic environment, and one that would be more suitable for children (they now have a small daughter, India). So, with customary flair and drama, the couple found a new home that had almost nothing in common with their docklands warehouse – a converted shop in a tiny cobbled street.

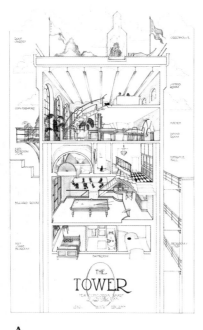

ABOVE: IN PRESERVING THE ORIGINAL structure of low-level storeys alternating with high ones, Piers Gough has remained faithful to the original fabric of the building, yet still created a unique and very workable living space.

RIGHT: TO THE LEFT OF THE KITCHEN IS A SMALL, INFORMAL SEATING CORNER filled with original Lloyd Loom furniture in charmingly faded colours. This cosy grouping has the distinct Art Deco atmosphere of the period that inspired the tower's overall look.

ABOVE: BEHIND THE STAIRWELL, AT THE OTHER END OF THE KITCHEN FROM THE
Lloyd Loom corner, is the much more formal dining area, which is lit by two
rows of tiny, ceiling-fixed tungsten halogen spotlights, plus candles on special
occasions. A plain white cloth covers the table, while diners sit on high-backed
chairs covered with a Liberty Arts and Crafts fabric.

ABOVE: TWO MODERN-DAY KNOLE SOFAS PILED WITH CUSHIONS PROVIDE ACRES
of comfortable seating in the top-level gallery, which is where Andrew and Julie
end up at the close of each day. The curtains are always left open to the tower's
spectacular views and the raging elements, from which its occupants, sitting in
front of a warm fire, feel well protected.

Developing Trends II
Fruit and Vegetable Shop

WITH APPEALING IRREVERENCE, THE GRANDEUR OF AN IMPOSING GEORGIAN TOWN HOUSE WAS RE-CREATED IN A COMPARATIVELY HUMBLE BUILDING THAT ONCE ACCOMMODATED A FLOURISHING GREENGROCERS

The property that Andrew Wadsworth and Julie Balmforth took on had a history that was diverse even for a couple accustomed to living in unusual places. Built in 1694, it was the result of an ingenious bit of seventeenth-century speculation whereby an aristocratic landowner, Sir Thomas Neale, granted a number of sixty-one year leases to individual builders. Each builder then put up a suitably-sized structure as quickly and cheaply as possible, and sold it on, at a profit, to an occupier who would finish it to suit his own taste and pocket. When the lease expired, the land and the buildings reverted to the original family, thus providing them with a developed estate for virtually no outlay.

The surrounding area, now fashionable and sought after, was then desperately poor, and the property's first occupants were probably itinerant weavers, who worked on the top storey and lived, in large numbers, on the floors below. A history of the house commissioned by Andrew revealed that, during its long life, it had accommodated up to thirty-seven people at a time, among them thieves, street-singers, bird-sellers, fish merchants and coster-mongers, many of whom would rent space on the floor by the night. During the first half of this century, the building was used as retail premises for, among other things, a greengrocery business. For several decades before the Wadsworths came on the scene however, it served only as warehousing space for a large firm of

RIGHT: JUST INSIDE THE FRONT DOOR, THE ENTRANCE AREA SETS THE SCENE FOR the rest of the house, with a cool, watery colour treatment, a late Arts and Crafts oak chair and hall stand, and beaten copper accessories.

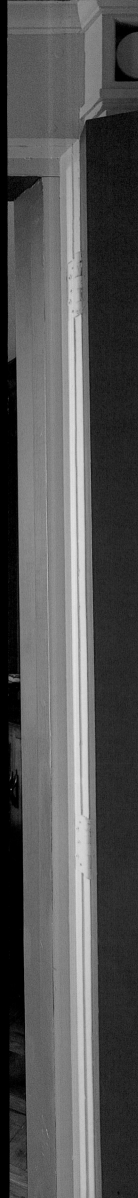

Right: WITH ITS green-and-cream scheme, wooden floor and simple tongue-and-groove units, the kitchen has an unpretentious look that reveals its Edwardian 'below stairs' inspiration. Above the deep, practical Butler sink, traditional brass taps are set into the wall, and even the stacked-up china has a distinctly church-hall feeling.

LEFT: IMMEDIATELY OFF the entrance hall, the dining room has been painted dark blue so its walls seem to disappear when the table is lit dramatically from above. Keeping watch at meal times is the statue of a fertility goddess, which Julie credits with the conception of her daughter India.

ironmongers who had traded in the area since the early part of the eighteenth century, and who owned much of the surrounding land. When they moved out, the local council was very anxious that at least part of the vacated area be used for housing, and was therefore very willing to approve any change-of-use schemes from commercial to residential. The Terry Farrell Partnership, the architectural firm in charge of the redevelopment, chose simply to make buildings like this stable, replacing roof, floors and walls where necessary. Most were then left as empty shells lined with plasterboard, awaiting the ideas and the resources of an imaginative buyer to bring them back to life.

This is the point at which Andrew and Julie arrived on the scene. Having sold their water tower – not surprisingly – to one of the first people who viewed it, they then had to find somewhere new to live. The process was not a drawn-out one; they saw the 'For Sale' sign, picked up the key from the agent nearby, and let themselves in. All they found was the empty box left by the developers, but they liked its size (very much smaller than the tower), its shape, and its general atmosphere, and they closed the deal there and then.

Curious to find out what lay behind the sheets of plasterboard, Andrew contacted Terry Farrell. As it turned out, the architect who had been in charge of the job, Stephen Ibbotson, had since left to set up his own company, but Farrell put them in touch with one another and Andrew, impressed with Ibbotson's wide knowledge of the building and the area, invited him to draw up a scheme for the interior. The brief was a wide one: to come up with a small-scale Georgian interior that would work as a comfortable family home. It was the 'Georgian' part that Ibbotson found slightly intimidating, since he was well aware how difficult it is to re-create a period style so that it looks right: a really authentic scheme is usually unconvincing to the modern eye because our visual perceptions of the past are often wildly inaccurate. His task was made more difficult by the fact that what Andrew had in mind was in fact rather cheeky – a modest artisan's house decorated in a grand manner that, although authentic in terms of date, bore no relation to the building's size or original style.

Steve's solution was to avoid a po-faced, academic approach and opt instead for an idiomatic, Georgian-*inspired* treatment that could never be mistaken for the real thing. By concentrating on the spirit rather than the letter of the chosen period, and on the intensity of ornamentation rather than its exact nature, he could also cope with having to scale down every column and cornice to suit the rooms'

RIGHT AND BELOW: THE WADSWORTH'S LIVING ROOM IS A TESTAMENT TO THEIR passion for the Arts and Crafts movement; the copper fireplace dates from 1904, and the candlesticks on top, also copper, were made by Christopher Dresser, an early industrial designer. (Tucked in the alcove is a rather later item – a Quentin Bell lampshade.) The coffee table is a brass-studded ship's chest that also provides storage space for India's toys: adult possessions are kept in a huge Liberty sideboard (below).

ABOVE: TRANSPORTED ALMOST INTACT FROM THEIR previous home (see page 57), the bathroom has gained a Victorian rocking chair and a pair of beautiful floor-length crewel-work curtains. Note how cleverly the cornice moulding becomes a pelmet, neatly concealing the curtain track.

comparatively diminutive proportions. What he came up with was a look that Andrew describes as 'compressed grandeur': every part of the house is rich in architectural detailing, with specially designed, deceptively complex, mouldings, panels and pilasters, yet the overall effect is never fussy or cluttered.

Interestingly, only the hammered brass ironmongery fitted throughout was salvaged from other buildings and re-used – everything else is new. Moreover, apart from traditional fibrous plaster, all the materials are modern ones like MDF (medium density fibreboard): unlike today's timber, this is as stable as the original, properly grown and aged, version would have been.

When it came to choosing colours, Andrew, Julie and Steve settled on two main schemes: the utilitarian, 'downstairs', areas like kitchen, bathroom and landing, are dark green and cream, while the more formal, 'upstairs', rooms have a royal blue, turquoise and eau de nil scheme very similar to the one in their previous home. Achieving the living room's subtle gradations of tone was a highly technical process: the three of them sat in the middle of the floor with pots of white paint and tubes of artists' colours, then mixed, dabbed, and mixed again until they got what they wanted. Polished boards covered with kelim rugs were their original choice underfoot, but this combination proved impractical for a small child, so they laid deep blue carpet instead.

Unlike the colour scheme, the furnishing style here is markedly different from that in the water tower. In fact, they sold much of their furniture with the tower, choosing instead to develop the Arts and Crafts theme that had worked so well in the small bedroom there. With typically impressive planning, Andrew and Julie collected suitable pieces and put them in storage for several months before they moved, so that when the house was finished, they were able to fill it almost immediately with the solid, late nineteenth-century, tables and chairs they had come to love.

In fact, nothing in this small but perfectly finished house is there by accident: every space and every surface has been meticulously considered and highly designed by architect, clients, or, more likely, a combination of both. Like Piers Gough, Steve Ibbotson found Andrew and Julie very rewarding patrons, exacting and demanding in their expectations, yet flexible and creative in approach, and highly appreciative when a tricky problem was solved or a difficult request filled. Looking at the result of this fruitful collaboration, it's tempting to wonder whether Sir Thomas Neale would approve.

RIGHT: LINING THE BASEMENT STAIRS, PURPOSE-BUILT SHELVES HOLD A collection that is somewhat less valuable than Andrew's Arts and Crafts furniture, yet just as appreciated by its owner – his tin boxes, canisters and biscuit barrels.

DRIVE AND VISION

ARMY GARAGES

IN A DRAMATIC ARCHITECTURAL *VOLTE-FACE*, A ROW OF SUBURBAN OUTBUILDINGS WENT FROM STORING MILITARY VEHICLES TO HOUSING A SUPERB COLLECTION OF TWENTIETH-CENTURY FINE AND APPLIED ART

Although any number of people yearn to live in an old barn or chapel, those whose fantasies involve a collection of derelict army garages in a city suburb must be rare indeed. To be fair, Bob McLaren did not set out to find such an extraordinary candidate for conversion; like many people who are emotionally involved with their homes, he bought it on a whim 'because it just felt right'. Sadly condemned by the local council by the time Bob found them, the buildings had begun their unorthodox history as coach houses attached to an imposing lodge. During World War II, the lodge was requisitioned by the military to provide headquarters for the Free French forces and their leader, Charles de Gaulle, and the coach houses were turned into accommodation for staff cars.

Although the space offered by the three double garages was generous, it was badly organized: there were seven different floor levels including a room above the centre garage that had once been a hay loft, and later a flat for the chauffeur. More than this however, the whole structure was in appalling condition, with almost no features worth preserving, so Bob began by gutting it, retaining only the original roof line and some of the gables, but lopping off their strangely Swiss-chaletish overhangs. He then gave the house a new front wall, bringing it out some distance from the original

RIGHT: HIDDEN FROM THE STREET BY A HIGH BRICK WALL, BOB MCLAREN'S front garden shows a strong Japanese influence, with its granite slabs and rectangular lily ponds. At the back, the steeply stepped flower beds are best viewed from this conservatory-like room (above left), filled with the innovative plywood furniture of the Finnish architect Alvar Aalto.

among others, plus several priceless Art Deco pieces, makes it look almost like a museum of contemporary applied art.

The atmosphere Bob McLaren has established however, is far from museum-like, and, in a way, its warmth and comfort surprised even him. 'I created the living space', he explains, 'partly as an exercise in style, partly to cope with the frustrations of doing a job that involves less and less actual design, and partly for the challenge of saving and making over a building that would otherwise have been demolished. When it was finished though, I felt really happy living here.' A medium once revealed to Bob that there were friendly spirits in residence; it may be that his home's previous occupants stamped it with their irrepressible *joie de vivre*.

Above: HUNG TO ALIGN WITH ONE OF THE LOW walls that give continuity to the building's many levels is an enormous, very stylized, poster portrait of Maurice Chevalier by Kiffer. The stairs on the left lead to the kitchen.

A CHANGE OF SCENE

FIELD BARN

USING HIS CONSIDERABLE EXPERIENCE DEVISING SETS FOR BALLET, OPERA AND FILMS, AN ADVENTUROUS TOWN DWELLER REFASHIONED AN OLD STONE BARN INTO A WELCOMING DOMESTIC AND PROFESSIONAL BASE

According to stage designer David Walker, purpose-built houses are incapable of fulfilling his domestic requirements simply because they were never designed to suit the needs of a single occupant. Converting an empty structure therefore, is the only way he can exercise complete control over the space in which he lives, works, and accommodates an unusually large number of visiting friends and relations. More than this though, he has always been intrigued by the idea of a building's evolution – of living in a place that has a diverse history of its own.

Typically, his previous home was a converted urban coach house; unlike many city dwellers, he was quite happy there and did not waste long hours fantasizing about an idyllic life in the country. When it came however, his decision to get away from the urban environment was sudden, and a childhood fascination with farm buildings led him to begin organizing his move by enquiring whether there were any barns for sale in his chosen area. Almost immediately, he was offered a suitable property: a large stone field barn plus small stables and a Dutch barn – one with open sides where the hay was dried. He knew at once that he could live in the main building, whereas the stables would be useful for storage, and the Dutch barn, when it had been knocked down, would provide space for a small, enclosed garden.

RIGHT: DAVID WALKER'S BACK DOOR WAS ONCE THE ENTRANCE TO THE BARN'S tack room, which is now his kitchen. On a sunny morning, the view looking in from the garden is so appealing that painter Barbara Dorf – a friend and frequent house guest of David's – was inspired to capture it in watercolour (above).

Aʙᴏᴠᴇ: ɪɴ ᴛʜᴇ ᴄᴀɴᴅʟᴇ-ʟɪᴛ ᴇɴᴛʀᴀɴᴄᴇ ʜᴀʟʟ, ᴠɪsɪᴛᴏʀs ᴀʀᴇ greeted by an eighteenth-century engraving of the actress Sarah Siddons. The oak chair is seventeenth century, as is the chest (also oak), which is covered with a Swedish cross-stitch runner from the middle of the last century.

Rɪɢʜᴛ: ᴛʜᴇ ʟᴀʀɢᴇ ʟᴀɴᴅɪɴɢ ᴏɴ ᴛʜᴇ ʟᴇᴠᴇʟ ᴏғ ᴛʜᴇ ᴏʀɪɢɪɴᴀʟ hay loft has become an inviting and comfortable sitting room. Against the far wall is a Regency signal cabinet; made to be used on board ship, this useful item of furniture is lined with pigeon-holes that once contained rolled-up flags. Next to the balustrade is a Victorian coaching table with crossed legs that fold up so it can be carried on long journeys.

When David took it on, his future house was only a shell, measuring about 13.5 × 7.5m (45 × 25ft), so its layout had to be planned from scratch. Because he was determined to retain existing features and divisions of space wherever possible, the level of the top floor is actually that of the hay loft. Similarly, the kitchen is located in the former tack room, its original entrance becoming the back door, while the three huge openings that provided access for the barn's bovine residents were preserved to become windows in the master bedroom.

More than anything though, David wanted the space in his home to flow so traffic would circulate naturally, leaving no area unused. The success of the wide staircase and large, gracefully proportioned rooms he designed with this in mind is demonstrated by the fact that, even when he is alone, there is never a day when he doesn't use every one of them. For variety, he made sure that each room differed in size, in height and in architectural details like the size and style of the windows, while through the centre of the house, linking it all together, he placed a chimney breast that serves the fireplaces in all the major rooms.

Once the plans were approved by the relevant authorities, he handed them over to a team of local craftsmen for execution; because he was putting the final touches to a production abroad at the time, he wasn't able to supervise their work, so he has had to put up with a number of mistakes, like windows in the wrong position. These things, however, he seems to have accepted philosophically. When he came back, he moved straight in, before the house had any ceilings, or plaster or − most importantly − heating. Such luxuries, along with furnishings and accessories, had to be acquired gradually, as money came in from an opera, a ballet, or the sale of one of his drawings.

David's decorating style is firmly rooted in previous centuries; now in his 50s, he considers himself to be part of the last generation for whom the past was not another country, but a living thing, handed on naturally in an undiluted form, not created artificially as a result of nostalgia. As a child during the war, he played with mostly nineteenth-century toys, cared for and handed down out of necessity, yet very much a part of everyday life. His father bought him original Pollocks toy theatres with their penny plain and tuppence coloured sheets, which sowed the first seeds of interest in his future career. Instead of films and adventure playgrounds, he

LEFT: A KASHMIRI SHAWL FROM THE 1840S IS DRAPED OVER THE SITTING room's linen-covered sofa. The desk and chair, both made in the eighteenth century, are oak. Tucked away on the floor is the Emmy award David was given for a television production of Hamlet that starred Richard Chamberlain.

ABOVE: ONE OF DAVID'S
ABOVE: ONE OF DAVID'S favourite places to work is in front of this large casement window that overlooks the surrounding hills. In addition to pens, brushes and inks, he surrounds himself with all the reference material he needs to re-create a particular style or period. The miniature dress form is used for constructing accurate quarter-scale patterns.

was taken to houses full of beautiful objects that inspired him even as early as three to begin drawing and making things. These influences were clearly strong ones: when recently a cousin came to visit that David had not seen for some years, he remarked that the atmosphere of the house was exactly the same one that David wove around himself in childhood.

In his view, there are two kinds of interiors: those that are created all at once to achieve a desired effect, and those that evolve naturally from the gradual accumulation of loved possessions. Although his rooms emphatically fall into the latter category, he professes to admire those that are elaborately 'decorated', at the same time admitting he would find it impossible to live in them. Furthermore, he can't abide being surrounded by the strong colours or the richly romantic atmosphere he creates on stage, so his chosen scheme is geared to induce a calm, restful environment. Apart from his bedroom, all the main rooms are clad in tongue-and-groove panelling painted with a soft grey-green eggshell finish that provides an ideal backdrop for the large collection of prints and

RIGHT: THE DINING room's candle chandelier was made for an eighteenth-century Swedish church, while behind the damask-covered table is a framed English fan from the same period. The chairs are Regency.

drawings of various styles, sizes and periods, whose subtlety he prefers to the more intense quality of paintings in oil or even watercolour.

His furniture consists mostly of pieces like those he grew up admiring, such as solid oak chests and tables, and many are the result of an abiding passion for auction rooms and antique shops. None of these things remain in the same place for very long, since David enjoys constantly re-arranging his house so he always sees it with a fresh eye. Nor does he have single, set purposes for any of his rooms; he doesn't even have an established place to work, but sets out his drawing board and inks wherever the fancy strikes him. This flexibility reflects the remarkable powers of concentration he has developed from having to work frequently in foreign hotel rooms, cramped airport lounges and draughty backstage nooks and crannies.

David values above all that which is appropriate, ordered and comfortable; his home is there to fill his needs, not vice-versa and he has neither the time, the patience nor the inclination to aim for contrived perfection in any of its elements. While appreciating his beautiful things deeply, David Walker, unlike Oscar Wilde and his celebrated blue china, has no intention of striving to live up to any of them.

RIGHT: THE bathroom's nautical theme is established by two unusual seascapes, both scenes of Portsmouth harbour during World War II painted by Margaret Ovey; next to these hangs a portrait of an anonymous naval commander. The classically-inspired medicine chest was made and decorated specially for David by his friend William Graham.

BELOW: IN HIS SUNNY white bedroom, David has kept the decorative elements to a minimum: a traditional quilt, a seventeenth-century oak headboard, and a charming 1930s screen, also by Margaret Ovey.

FRIENDLY PERSUASION
QUAKER MEETING HOUSE

WHEN A SPACIOUS, AND ENCHANTINGLY SIMPLE, WOODEN BUILDING WAS NO LONGER USED FOR WEEKLY SERVICES, IT NEEDED LITTLE ALTERATION TO BECOME THE HEART OF A COSY FAMILY HOME

The same remarkable family that produced the poet Robert Browning sprouted an American branch at about the same time, and Elizabeth Browning Jackson, a busy furniture and textile designer, is a member of this clan. The New World Brownings were Quakers, and this heritage has always been important to Elizabeth, so when she and her husband Peter Allen were casting around for a sanctuary from the frenzy of New York City, they were greatly intrigued when someone they knew told them about a Friends meeting house in New England that was being auctioned by the sect to raise money for other congregations. (Showing similar respect for her famous family, she named her baby daughter Barrett.) Apart from its associations, the building seduced the couple on sight with its proximity to the sea, its surrounding grain fields, and its very reasonable condition – a slight surprise since it had lain empty for nearly fifty years.

Elizabeth's overriding instinct was to leave the interior untouched; never de-consecrated, it had a very special, peaceful atmosphere worth preserving. In addition, the 'open stone' foundation (it is literally like a horizontal wall of stones), although allowing air to circulate and keep the building dry, made laying on a water supply impossible. So, to serve their practical needs Elizabeth and Peter erected an almost identical extension that

RIGHT: BENEATH PENDANT LAMPS THAT ONCE ILLUMINATED QUAKER MEETINGS, the main room has been decorated in suitably episcopal colours. The dining furniture is antique (some of the chairs are Chippendale), while in the living area, the boxy 20s seating is by Josef Hoffmann and the linked unit came from an old synagogue – in its base are storage compartments for hats.

contains the kitchen, bathrooms and additional bedrooms, thus freeing the meeting house itself to become an open-plan living and dining area, with a narrow bedroom that overlooks it tucked away in the choir loft.

When the extension was finished, their sympathetic builder fitted the appropriate architectural detailing, meticulously copied from the old building. All that was left for the owners to do was add a coat of white paint, pick out the woodwork in subtle shades of grey, and attach to every window shutters made from cheap pegboard, yet fashioned meticulously by Peter to his own design. To echo the existing external shutters, these are divided so that the top section is permanently fixed and only the bottom can be opened. This unsophisticated window treatment, like the rest of the house, has the strong Shaker qualities of simplicity, practicality and fine craftsmanship; similarly, the family hang their coats and hats on the original, very Shakerish, peg rail in the hall. (Also extremely useful is the old outhouse, with its doors still designated 'Boys' and 'Girls', which makes a perfect home for gardening equipment.)

When it came to furnishing style, their choice was a necessarily eclectic mix of antiques (largely inherited from Elizabeth's grandmother) and contemporary pieces, either modern classics or Elizabeth's own designs. In this cheerful jumble, her colourful, witty rugs lie next to traditional pencil-post beds, and a painted toy chest sits on top of a valuable Persian carpet. Nevertheless, just as Elizabeth and Peter intended, the effect is an uncommonly tranquil one in which her Quaker forbears would be very happy.

ABOVE: THE HUGE, EXQUISITELY CRAFTED cupboard that now holds crockery and glasses once opened out to reveal the altar. When she first looked inside, Elizabeth found a prayer book, a hymnal, and a detailed log recording information about the brethren.

LEFT: SQUEEZED INTO THE CHOIR LOFT ABOVE THE original meeting hall, this corridor-shaped bedroom contains two heirloom pencil-post beds separated by one of Elizabeth's rugs. On the left, behind an English military chest, are her grandmother's Louis Vuitton suitcases; now treasured by everyone, they were once despised, and very nearly got thrown away.

RIGHT: AS A DRAMATIC CONTRAST, THE KITCHEN has a strong 50s atmosphere with its stainless steel units and black floor and work surfaces. Several of the designs in this room are Elizabeth's own, like the rug, the cantilevered chairs and the ingenious plate rack, built into the counter with drainage holes underneath. On the left, an old wood-and-metal pie safe links this era to the earlier periods suggested elsewhere in the house.

A TRIUMPH OF STYLE

TRIUMPHAL ARCH

ONE RESOURCEFUL MODERN ARCHITECT HAS A BRILLIANT
EIGHTEENTH-CENTURY COLLEAGUE TO THANK FOR HIS WEEKEND
RETREAT IN A UNIQUE AND HISTORIC FOLLY

When Thomas Coke (later first Earl of Leicester) invited visitors to his family seat, Holkham Hall, he made sure their approach to it was carefully orchestrated. At the end of a long, straight drive, fully two miles from the great Palladian house, he erected an imposing Triumphal Arch to act as a southern gateway to the estate, and give travellers a foretaste of the grandeur of Holkham itself.

Designed in the 1730s by William Kent, and constructed, together with the main house, over a period of thirty years, the Arch (actually one large arch flanked by two smaller ones) was built in the rustic Doric style, derived from Palladio's fashionable reinterpretation of ancient Roman architecture.

Since the nineteenth century, visitors have come increasingly to use the northern entrance to the Hall, so the once-grand Arch fell into disrepair. Enter architect Nicholas Hills, a specialist in country house renovation and design, who happened on the sorry structure during a holiday in the area. Enchanted by the idea of living in such a place, he wrote to the late Earl to enquire whether it was available to rent; once Hills' references had been thoroughly checked and approved the Earl agreed.

As a home, the building had many drawbacks: apart from being in a ruinous state, it had no water or electricity. The massive stonework exterior was solid though, and the craftsmanship and detailing were superb, thanks to Kent's chief architect, Matthew

RIGHT: THE ARCH REPRESENTS A LEVEL OF WORKMANSHIP IMPOSSIBLE TO duplicate today: not only were all its bricks fired on the estate, but the ones in the side arches are smaller than those in the central arch, and the tiny pieces of inset flint are smaller too, each one fitting like pieces of a jigsaw. Above, a portrait of Matthew Brettingham with a sketch of his project.

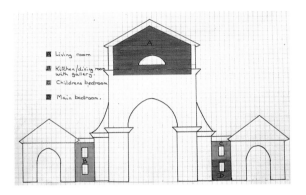

ABOVE: IN NICHOLAS HILLS' PLAN, THE LIVING ROOM spans the central arch, so its original semi-circular windows offer spectacular views over the drive leading to the main house.

Brettingham. It's clear from Kent's drawings that he intended the Arch mainly for decorative purposes, but Brettingham made several changes, such as enlarging the windows and increasing their number, that made it more suitable for habitation. This may have been because he wanted it to be used as a picnic or hunting lodge, since Hills discovered evidence of such a function during rebuilding: swept under the floorboards was an assortment of eighteenth-century litter in the form of china fragments, oyster shells, mutton bones and broken claret bottles.

Although Hills had plumbing and drainage laid on, there is still no electricity (he's considering a wind generator), and the only sources of heat are a wood fire and a collection of oil lamps which, astonishingly, provide over a kilowatt of heat in addition to 40 watts of light.

The building's largest room – what Hills calls the saloon – is the chamber over the main arch measuring about 3.6×7.2m (12×24ft), into which a stone staircase rises from a lofty kitchen in one of the wings. Above this kitchen, a recently installed gallery houses a dressing room/storage area, plus a bathroom. The other wing, which has access only from the outside, comprises two bedrooms for children and guests, and a second bathroom. It's around the saloon however, that the household is centred, since Hills and his wife live, sleep and entertain there.

A beautiful room with spectacular views in four directions, this space was open right up to the roof when Hills arrived, the ceiling having been one of the casualties of years of neglect. The airy, soaring feeling this gave impressed him so much that he left it the way it was, fixing insulation between the old rafters and the new ones he added, then covering this with plasterboard. The bare brick walls – any plaster fell off decades ago – were painted cream; there's little danger of draughts since they're 60cm (2ft) thick.

Once the room was decorated, a new set of problems presented itself. The only way to get furniture in was via the narrow staircase, so, where possible, large pieces were dismantled and re-assembled *in situ*. Sleeping and seating facilities were still a problem though, until Hills came up with a clever design for a round bed made from four wedges of foam covered with a feather squab. During the day, this folds up to make a semi-circular sofa that reflects the shape of the beautiful arched window behind it, one of two that were Brettingham additions. To display these to best advantage, natural

RIGHT: VIEWED THROUGH THE DOOR INTO THE WESTERN ARCH, THE DINING room and kitchen are lit by candles, plus a storm pendant lantern copied from one on the estate; bottled gas and a solid fuel stove provide heat for cooking. The gallery above, added by Hills, contains dressing and shower rooms.

cotton curtains hung from simple wooden poles are held completely clear with tie-backs of silken cord. On either side of the sofa
bed stand matching bookcases, which Hills designed and commissioned. Their shape, an allusion to the Kent obelisks along the
drive, accommodates books of all sizes plus, in their bases, a
battery-operated car radio and television.

Even with all the resourcefulness and style Hills has invested in
his Arch, few people would find it a convenient place to live: the
novelty of collecting wood, splitting logs, cleaning grates and
filling lamps – as well as keeping the resulting grime at bay – could
soon wear thin. But as far as he's concerned, there are more than
enough compensations. Apart from the cattle grazing nearby
(sometimes near enough to trample garden furniture), nothing
disturbs the extraordinary atmosphere of peace and security in and
around this beautiful building. It's easy for him to understand why
Lord Chief Justice Coke, who established the fortune on which
Holkham was built, was moved to make the celebrated observation
that, 'an Englishman's home is unto him as his castle or his fortress'.

RIGHT: ABOVE BOTH LARGE WINDOWS IN THE MAIN ROOM, HILLS HAS FIXED HUGE
stag antlers; found at a country house sale, these hint at the arch's early role as a
hunting lodge. Prints of other arches, and busts of Homer and the Belvedere
Apollo all pay homage to the classical inspiration of its architecture.

BELOW: AT NIGHT, THE ROOM GLOWS IN THE LIGHT FROM CANDLES, OIL LAMPS,
and a twelve-branch central candelabrum. The obelisk bookcases were made in
four sections, so they could not only be transported by car, but also carried up
the exceptionally narrow stairs.

A FIGHTING
SPIRIT

MARTELLO TOWER

NEVER UTILIZED FOR ITS INTENDED PURPOSE, A MASSIVE COASTAL
FORTIFICATION WAS NOT FULLY OCCUPIED AND PROPERLY
APPRECIATED UNTIL NEARLY 200 YEARS AFTER ITS CONSTRUCTION

Stretched out one summer's day on a pebbly beach, John and
Suzanne Fell-Clark were discussing their current housing
problems. They had to give up their beautiful Elizabethan manor
house nearby, from which John also ran his international antiques
business, since he needed a more central base. Unwilling to leave
the countryside altogether, they drew up a list of requirements for a
weekend base; in essence, they wanted a property by the sea, but
one that was unusual and challenging. In the distance, John caught
sight of a massive brick edifice with a roundish, rather dumpy
shape. 'There you are', he said to Suzanne flippantly, 'we can live in
that'. As soon as the words were spoken, they both realized how
appealing this prospect seemed, and set out to investigate.

What they had found was a Martello tower, one of 103 built in
the early years of the nineteenth century. The name is a corruption
of Mortella Point, the site of a similar tower on the island of
Corsica, which was captured by Napoleon's forces in 1793. The
Corsicans called on the English for help, and although their
response was immediate, they had to bombard the structure
heavily three times before it fell. Deeply impressed, the Ministry of
Defence commissioned similar fortifications to be built along the
southern and eastern coastlines in case of invasion by the common
enemy. In the event, they never saw a shot fired in anger, although

RIGHT: DESPITE THE ABSENCE OF WINDOWS ON THE GROUND FLOOR, A
surprising amount of light streams in through the stairwell, reflected off the sea
and the tower's white walls. The handrail and balustrade are made from
scaffolding and yacht rigging respectively. Originally erected in groups of four,
the Martello towers (above) each contain about 750,000 bricks.

Victorian revenue men used them to keep watch for smugglers and, during both World Wars, they served as lookouts for enemy aircraft. By the end of the last war, there were only about forty Martello towers left, and these were mostly given or sold off cheaply to the owners of the land they stood on.

Once John and Suzanne discovered these fascinating architectural specimens, their interest quickly became an obsession, and one that brought them up against countless obstacles. To begin with, many of the towers, like the one they first spotted, were not for sale. Moreover, those that were available were either in built-up or unattractive areas, or so remote that it would have been impossible to reach them even by car, let alone lay on power and water. Against all odds, they finally found one that was perfect; although derelict, it was virtually on a beach and reasonably isolated, yet near to two other buildings (a holiday bungalow and a hunting lodge) that already had the necessary access and services. The land was owned by a farmer, to whom they immediately put in an offer, subject to planning permission for conversion to domestic use. Unfortunately, he had given the tower to his daughter who, although she had no plans to develop it herself, refused to sell. The Fell-Clarks had no intention of giving up however, and spent the whole of the next year persuading her to reconsider. Finally, she succumbed, and plans for the alterations were drawn up to be submitted to the planning department of the local authority. The officials there were helpful, encouraging and efficient, but sadly, they were not the only interested parties.

After years of neglect, Martello towers had begun to attract the attention of English Heritage, the advisory body on buildings of historical importance, who listed them as 'ancient monuments' and set down a great many strict regulations governing any changes that could be made. They immediately rejected John and Suzanne's plans, which had included a door and several windows at ground level (where there were neither) on the basis that the exterior should not be touched. A completely new set of plans was presented, but the episode took on an element of farce when English Heritage's requirements directly contradicted the quite sensible local planning regulations concerning minimum size and number of doors and windows. It seemed that this second group of civil servants would rather see the tower fall to ruin than reach a reasonable compromise. In the end, the local authority gave way in order to ensure the building's preservation.

The next problem was a financial one: because adhering to the relevant guidelines would involve a large additional cash outlay, English Heritage agreed to give John a grant to cover 30 per cent of the renovation cost. On this understanding, he completed the

Aᴃᴏᴠᴇ: CONSTRUCTED FROM SOLID BRICKWORK with no rubble, the walls at their thickest measure nearly 3m (9ft). A special sealant was fitted around all the windows to counteract draughts.

Rɪɢʜᴛ: ON THE UPPER LEVEL, ADDITIONAL LIGHTING is provided by four halogen lamps positioned around the central column. Choosing furniture for the tower was extremely difficult, since every item had to be small enough to go up the outside staircase, yet heavy enough visually so it wasn't swamped by the structure's titanic proportions. Both these requirements are satisfied by the seventeenth-century oak coffer near the kitchen, and the antique yew table with its rustic styling and tripod construction.

ABOVE: A WEDGE-SHAPED AREA OF FLAGSTONES makes up one quarter of the tower's upper floor; in the main fireside seating area, a bright red rug adds visual and actual warmth. Just visible are two Italian Bambole sofas designed by Mario Bellini and covered with reverse buffalo hide.

purchase, and expected to begin work. When it came to collecting his grant however, he had no success, even after countless phone calls. Eventually, they confirmed that he was indeed eligible – but they were sorry, they had run out of money.

At this point, the couple had no choice but to launch into the conversion anyway, and hope for the best. Basically, the walls were sound (since they're 2.75m [9ft] thick in some places, this was not surprising), but a great deal of water had found its way in through the flagstone-covered roof that was originally a sunken battlement on the top of the tower. Inside, many of the bricks had crumbled away, and others were covered with lime deposits. The first task was to repair the roof and renew the missing 15–23cm (6–9in) flagstones, and once that was done, all the damaged bricks were either replaced or cleaned and repointed. Getting rid of the damp though, was a longer-term proposition; over a period of three months, two industrial dehumidifiers removed 4500 litres (1000 gallons) of water and, even now, a small machine stays on all the time. To allow any remaining moisture to evaporate, the bricks had to be covered with a porous whitewash mixed from lime and tallow, rather than ordinary paint, which is largely impervious. Happily, ventilation was taken care of by the original builders, who ducted every alcove and window casement into the roof to cope with the cordite given off from exploding gunpowder.

The tower's earth base was concreted over, and an under-floor electric heating system set into the screed on top. The upper level was originally supported by massive oak joists radiating out from the central supporting column; on top of these, linking them together, 2.5cm (1in) thick boards, also oak, had been laid spider's-web fashion. All this had to be replaced, but the new floor was constructed in exactly the same way, using jarrah – an Australian timber – instead of oak, which would have been too expensive.

When it came to planning the layout of the tower, John and Suzanne decided to preserve its original form by keeping partition walls to a minimum. On the ground floor, the bathroom, toilet and utility room are sited in what used to be the powder magazine, with water, drainage and ventilation channels running under the floor, through part of a sunken, wedge-shaped cistern that was intended to collect rainwater. (The remainder of this chamber has been put to rather more glamorous use as a jacuzzi.) Since English Heritage had forbidden *any* drilling through the wall, getting this pipework to the outside could have posed a problem. Fortuitously though, vandals had already knocked a big enough hole nearby.

The Fell-Clark's two children occupy separate bedrooms that take up large alcoves, also on the ground floor. The rest of this level is open, and takes in the stairwell and occasional sleeping quarters

ABOVE: THE DINING table's elegant top is a piece of early nineteenth-century marble; the base is a concrete drain pipe. Modern tubular chairs stack away when they're not required. For the kitchen, John and Suzanne commissioned custom-made units that fit accurately around the curved walls, but they settled for carefully chosen freestanding domestic appliances rather than the more expensive built-in variety. On the wall is a sixteenth-century Flemish tapestry.

for guests, which can be partitioned off with a sliding door.

The upper storey (which is where you come in) constitutes a sort of giant bed-sitting room for John and Suzanne, their mattress folding down from a cupboard in the living area. Directly over the sunken cistern on the lower floor, the kitchen runs along the curved wall, so its water and waste pipes can tuck inside the shafts that were built to carry rainwater from the roof. The focal point of this space is an enormous original fireplace, which is in constant use; in front of it, flagstones had been laid to protect the magazine below from sparks, and these too have been restored. From this level, leading up to a roof terrace, are two flights of stairs, one on each side, whose exits are protected by a conservatory that spans them both.

In many ways, the Martello towers that were conceived so long ago are a sad waste of materials, technology and the enormous energy it must have taken to build them; never used for their original, proud, purpose, most of them have crumbled away ignominiously, or been carelessly destroyed. If it weren't for the incredible tenacity of John and Suzanne Fell-Clark, this one too would almost certainly have been lost. They are profoundly grateful though that their obsession drove them on when giving up seemed the only sensible thing to do, for last thing at night, gazing up at the vaulted ceiling lit by their dying fire, they cannot imagine any other home that could give its owners as much joy.

STABLE
MANNERS

TACK ROOM AND STABLES

TRANSFORMING A DANK UNDERGROUND CHAMBER INTO AN
ELEGANT AND INVITING HOUSE WOULD SEEM TO REQUIRE THE KIND
OF WIZARDRY USUALLY ASSOCIATED WITH MAGIC WORDS AND
PUFFS OF SMOKE

W hen most people set off in search of a new home, they list things
like a fitted kitchen, a big garden, or proximity to local shops as
their major requirement. For Felicity Dahl however, the main
priority was something much more basic, and certainly more
difficult to achieve – perfect proportions. If this hadn't been the
case, it's unlikely she'd have ended up with a mid-Victorian tack
room and stables – a cavernous, damp, semi-subterranean space
that had nothing to offer *except* its proportions.

Felicity (usually known as Liccy, pronounced Lissy) first saw the
building when she went in search of premises for a crafts workshop
she had helped to set up. She discovered an intriguing 'To Let' sign
on a property in a decaying and dirty mews, but by the time she had
contacted the estate agent to make enquiries, it had been sold.
Nonetheless, her interest had been caught, and when she returned
to the mews to have another look, she was amazed to find that all
the buildings were empty except one, whose internal shape, viewed
through bars and grimy glass, appeared to meet her standards. On
inquiring, she discovered that it, along with the rest of the mews,
was owned by the local council, whose historical department was
using it for storage – a piece of information that explained the
jumble of crates, boxes and bits of architectural salvage inside.

R IGHT: A HUGE ENGLISH ROCOCO MIRROR BY MATHIAS LOCK HANGS OVER A
Georgian sofa near the gallery-level bedroom, while a small-scale relative with the
same eighteenth-century origins lives by the front door (above). Behind the
display table is a Chippendale chair that belonged to Liccy's father, a celebrated
thoracic surgeon who rejoiced in the name Alphonsus Ligori Pon d'Abreu.

ABOVE: IN THE KITCHEN, LICCY FACED BOTH WALLS and storage shelves with white ceramic tiles, a practical idea that she first picked up in France. Planned so each surface and appliance is positioned in the best order for use, the room has a galley shape that is made slightly less extreme by the deep marble surface running under the window; commissioned to be part of a monument to John Paul Getty, but never collected, this was sold off cheaply for its present, more prosaic, use.

When the council was later disbanded, the whole thing was put up for tender; coincidentally, it was bought by someone who knew of Liccy's interest, and asked if she still wanted the building she had seen originally. By this time, the workshop had found a home, but Liccy, recently divorced from her first husband, was very much in need of one, so she bravely accepted the challenge and set out with the aim of turning it into a comfortable and elegant home. She faced her first setback in the form of an exhausting series of battles with the local planning authority, but she stood her ground, and eventually contracts were exchanged.

Wisely realizing the scope of what she had taken on, she enlisted the help of her brother-in-law, Marius Barron, an architect who specializes in the renovation of period buildings; what they faced was an unsavoury hole devoid of even plumbing or wiring. Although it had been used as an upholstery workshop before World War II, the entrance had never been altered, so this consisted simply of a wide ramp down which the horses would have been led, through what is now the kitchen, to the floor level 1.6m (6ft) below. Inside they found two huge pillars, a recessed water trough, and an alarming amount of water seeping up from a small stream below. It was at this stage that most of her friends – and all her builders – let her know they thought she was completely mad.

That notwithstanding, Liccy instantly saw the finished plan in her mind: a new, centrally placed, entrance would lead down to a large, open living area with a gallery added above it – something she had always wanted. All the other rooms – bedrooms, bathroom, kitchen and study – would fit in, one above the other, on either side. Almost coincidentally, this layout resulted in a main room that was a nearly perfect 6m (19ft) square.

Before work could begin though, all traces of damp had to be eradicated, and this was done by installing not only a standard damp-proof course, but also an ingenious tanking system that took the form of a sort of upside-down swimming pool. The next major problem was one of noise; above the ceiling beams, there were only thin floorboards, so a layer of soundproofing had to be fitted behind a false ceiling. Fortunately though, the beams were thick enough to stand proud of this, their unusual grid pattern adding interest to the rooms below.

When it came to decoration and furnishing, architect and client agreed that the early Georgian period should provide their inspiration; apart from being a favourite with both of them, this style seemed to be exactly right for the building, despite its slightly later date. To display Liccy's beautiful furniture most effectively, they chose a soft grey scheme, graded, in the manner of the time, from a white ceiling, through softly tinted walls, to a subtle medium tone

on the skirting boards. In the living room, the main seating area is defined with a specially woven rug that features a key pattern border in matching grey. Underneath this, the floorboards, like all the woodwork in the house including the kitchen units and the turned handrail on the stairs, are of pale Douglas fir, chosen for its practicality as well as its warm glow. Rejecting even the idea of polyurethane, Liccy insisted on waxing every inch of it by hand, thus providing her bemused builder with further evidence that his client was not altogether in possession of her faculties.

To avoid a jarring twentieth-century note, heat is provided by traditional cast-iron radiators partially concealed under the deep window seats. The simplest of Austrian blinds in white calico afford privacy, yet cut out the minimum of light; in addition, they reveal the shape of the windows, which, naturally, have close to ideally Georgian proportions. At night, gentle, indirect illumination comes from recessed spots supplemented by table lights.

Although Liccy moved into her lovingly created home as a single person, it has become very much a family dwelling, first because she was married from here – to her present husband, the writer Roald Dahl – and later on account of the endless parade of children (they have seven between them) that passes through. Her spirited decision to take on such a mammoth restoration project could easily have brought disappointment; instead it marked the beginning of a new and extremely happy chapter in her life.

ABOVE: UNUSUALLY COSY IN ATMOSPHERE, THE bathroom is decorated with rows of family photographs, including a large one of Liccy's husband Roald. Behind the ticking-covered day-bed, an old Boldings sink is mounted on a brass stand that serves an equally useful function as a towel rail.

REFORMED CHAPEL

METHODIST CHAPEL

A CREATIVE COUPLE'S RIGID REQUIREMENTS CONCERNING THE LOCATION AND SIZE OF THEIR COUNTRY HOME, AS WELL AS ITS APPEARANCE, WERE EASILY MET BY A CHARMING, BUT REDUNDANT, VILLAGE CHURCH

During their early years together, Doug Patterson and Joanna Buxton did not list owning and improving a home among their top priorities; their main enthusiasm was travel, so all available time and money was devoted to exploring far-away places, and they returned only to catch their breath and earn enough to set off again. After several years of this hectic hurtling around the globe however, they decided to spend a summer at home, and were able to borrow a house in the countryside where they could escape for weekends. By the time autumn came, Doug and Jo had been completely seduced by the tranquillity and charm of rural life, and from then on their energies were concentrated on finding a country home of their own.

Trained as an architect, Doug is now a partner in the design consultancy Patterson Hewitt, but much of his spare time is spent drawing and painting bizarre buildings from all over the world; Jo is a tapestry weaver and designer. Since these pursuits are carried on in separate town studios during the week, they wanted most of all to have a single working space large enough to accommodate both of them at weekends. Jo's hulking loom had to be found house room as well, so a purpose-built dwelling was out of the question, and they realized they would have to convert a larger building of some kind.

RIGHT: THE CHAPEL'S ORIGINAL ARCHED DOOR AND WINDOWS (SEE ABOVE FOR outside view) frame exceedingly pretty views of the village green and allow plenty of light to flood into the soaring interior. At night, the room is illuminated by wall fittings that are actually bed-head reading lights, made in the 1930s by Best & Lloyd for the Savoy hotel apartments.

Recognizing that a chapel would fill their needs perfectly, Doug wrote off to the Methodist Church to ask whether they knew of any that were available, and they directed him to a pretty village green where a suitable building was by then in use only as a Sunday school. He made an offer to the managing agent, but before this could be accepted the chapel's availability had to be publicized since, as a charity, the Church was obliged to make sure they had the highest possible bid. Happily, there were no other offers, and Doug's was accepted.

Having achieved their main requirement of a large living and working area, Doug and Jo still had to find room for a kitchen and bathroom, and the logical solution was to build a small extension, which they had every intention of doing. Doug drew up plans, but before work had begun, they were given the chance to buy the cottage next door, which was actually attached to the chapel, even though it had no direct access. In terms of space, this could scarcely have been more ideal, so new plans were drawn up for the conversion of the two properties, both of them virtually derelict.

The work was done in three main stages: first, the chapel's roof was removed and the structure was completely rebuilt. When this had been done, the roof was re-battened and felted, and the original tiles replaced. Inside, Doug added a gallery bedroom, which is linked by a spiral staircase to the studio below. Next, the cottage was similarly demolished and reconstructed to provide a kitchen and dining area on the ground floor, with a guest bedroom and bathroom above. Here again, the original pantiled roof was salvaged and reinstated. Heat for all the rooms comes from a propane gas boiler; because of the buildings' exposed location, Doug dry lined the walls to make sure they were well insulated. Despite the large expanses of glass, draughts are not a problem either, since the windows are extremely well fitted. This is particularly surprising in view of the fact that many of them, in common with several other architectural elements and most of the internal fittings, were rescued from demolition sites and salvage yards all over the country, then fitted by a sympathetic builder.

The final stage of construction took the form of a small tower added on to the back of the chapel; this contains a sunny garden room with a small bathroom on top leading off the sleeping gallery.

From the beginning, Doug and Jo decided on a clean, uncluttered style for their country home, both to take advantage of its

LEFT: AT THE OTHER END OF THE MAIN ROOM IS A SMALL GALLERY BEDROOM with its own bathroom beyond. This structure (including the balustrade, which was rescued from a demolition site) is supported by fibrous plaster columns. On the floor, simple tongue-and-groove boards are protected with yacht varnish.

LEFT: THE KITCHEN'S trefoil window comes from a redundant country school, while the work surfaces are pieces of marble cladding from an inner-city demolition site. Tough ceramic floor tiles complete a fresh-looking all-white scheme.

unusual shape and interesting detailing, and to provide contrast to a city flat full of clutter that has been accumulating since their student days. In addition, they wanted a timeless environment, free of fashionable design gimmicks that would date quickly or, more importantly, that they would tire of. To achieve this, they filled the spare, modern, white-painted rooms with solid, traditional pieces of furniture, many of them large and architectural in feeling. The couple's scavenging instincts are again evident in the fact that most of these came from house clearances and sale or auction rooms rather than expensive antique shops. All the building and furnishing materials are natural ones, their largely subtle tones relieved by the vivid colour of a fabric, a rug, a picture, or a bunch of flowers.

Doug's obsession with buildings and their elements is obvious from both the architectural drawings displayed in every part of the house, and his huge and disparate collection of columns of every size and shape, from massive specimens holding up the gallery, to slender ones that act as lamp bases. A refreshing streak of irreverence is demonstrated by the sprinkling of blatant fakes – 'marble' sculptures made of resin, or well-known pictures that are only inexpensive prints.

It's clear that Doug and Jo have enjoyed restoring their chapel home and filling it with things they love, some of which might, without them, have been lost forever. They do not, however, fall into that category of people who, once a property is 'done-up', lose interest and set off in search of another wreck. The restlessness of their youth has in no way been dissipated and they still travel whenever they have the opportunity, but these days they tend to return contentedly to their home, fired with exciting new ideas for the house on which they have lavished so much affection.

RIGHT: FOR THE dining room (adjoining the kitchen), Doug and Jo have chosen a decorating theme of fruit, flowers and food, plus their signature columns, here in the form of alabaster lamp bases and a carved wooden mirror surround. The chequerboard floor, which looks black and white, is actually in subtler shades of beige and charcoal.

Above: DOMINATING THE SOFT-PINK BEDROOM IS A DECEPTIVELY INTRICATE QUILT; OLD AND expensive looking at first glance, it was actually mass produced in Portugal and bought very cheaply. Another thrifty purchase was the unusual semi-circular window, which began its life in a railway station.

Right: LIKE THE LIVING ROOM'S WALL LIGHTS, EVERYTHING IN THE BATHROOM – DOORS, ironmongery, sanitary fittings and taps – came from the Savoy apartments. The trefoil windows have the same pedigree as the one in the kitchen, and the walls are covered with grey marble slips alternated with standard white ceramic tiles.

FACTORY RESULTS
METAL COMPONENTS FACTORY

WHEN THEY HAD SUCCEEDED IN CARVING HABITABLE LIVING
QUARTERS OUT OF A COLLAPSING INDUSTRIAL BUILDING, ITS
OCCUPANTS GAVE IT A SURPRISING – AND STUNNINGLY SUCCESSFUL –
COLOUR TREATMENT

It's not so much that Philippe and Cécile Pradalie are enamoured of living in converted industrial buildings; it's more that they don't feel they have any choice, in that few purpose-built houses – and even fewer in the very central area of Paris where they want to be – are large enough to suit them. As well as three active sons, who take up considerable room by themselves, the couple need vast amounts of studio and office space, since they both work at home: he is a painter and art teacher, while she is a graphic designer whose broadly based portfolio includes everything from fashion and furnishing textiles to wallcoverings and wrapping paper.

Although they were already living in a similar warehouse conversion when they found this turn-of-the-century metal components factory, they had rapidly outgrown it. They were delighted therefore to find a property that had the industrial-sized spaces they so desperately needed extending over two floors – a very unusual arrangement, but one that suited them perfectly. Unfortunately, there were drawbacks. First, the locality was far from chic – in fact it was positively disreputable – but the Pradalie family came to grips with this fairly easily. Much more seriously, the building was so close to collapse that they had to work on it for an entire year before a single floor was habitable. Even when

RIGHT: DISPLAYED AGAINST THE GENTLE PINK OF THE WALLS IS A GROUP OF objects the Pradalies have inherited or collected from flea markets: the three small boxes were made by the children, while the oval portrait is of their grandfather as a boy. As well as offering vast amounts of space, the factory (above) also provides a wall of windows for maximum light.

ABOVE: PHILIPPE AND CÉCILE HAVE GROWN AN impressive collection of plants from seedlings; in every possible shape and size, these define areas of activity as well as supply a welcome touch of greenery in an unmistakably urban environment.

RIGHT: PHILIPPE PRADALIE NOT ONLY MADE THE simple, but extremely practical work drawers that contain Cécile's designs, he also painted the portrait of her with their children that hangs above it.

pressed, it's difficult for them to fix on any one thing that went wrong. 'It was all absolutely terrible', states Cécile with that air of finality people employ when the conversation strays on to subjects too painful for them to contemplate. The fact that the whole renovation took eight years to complete suggests that her reticence is more than justified.

Discussing the *appartement* in its present form however, she is full of affection and enthusiasm, since the dank, crumbling shell they took on has been transformed into a home that is full of light and warmth. Although the couple insisted on an open-plan layout rather than rigid living and working areas, the overwhelming atmosphere is cosy and inviting, with each space flowing naturally into the next, separated only by a group of plants, a row of widely spaced uprights made from old planks, or an imposing piece of furniture. Linking all the 'rooms' together is a common colour theme of shell pink, a surprising choice given the strongly architectural character of the building. With their collectively heightened visual sense however, they realized that this shade, far from being suitable only for frilly boudoirs, is an inspired choice for any room, since it enhances all kinds of light, from streaming sun to subtle artificial illumination, so that every corner is continually bathed in a soft, flattering glow. Reinforcing this luminous effect are the polished wooden floors, constructed from a carefully chosen variety of beautifully toned woods that, as a bonus, are equally sympathetic to both living and working areas, extremely hard-wearing and easy to look after.

When it came to furnishings, Philippe and Cécile resisted the temptation to cram in as many things as possible, choosing instead to create small, isolated, groupings of pictures and flowers displayed with the silver, glass and porcelain pieces they have collected from flea markets. Their almost exclusively antique furniture provides a lively contrast to Philippe's paintings which, although strictly representational in approach, are uncompromisingly modern in style.

Many people would have found it impossible to cope with the plethora of problems faced by the Pradalies: the easiest solution for them would have been either to make do, finding separate work and living quarters, or put up with cramped conditions that were bound to lead to constant irritation and inconvenience as well as impose severe limitations on both their personal and professional lives. By sheer effort of will however, combined with endless hard work and infinite imagination, this couple have achieved what at one time seemed impossible – they have fulfilled every one of their housing requirements, and fashioned a home of exceptional charm at the same time.

OPEN PLANS I
VICTORIAN WAREHOUSE

SPACE IS THE MAIN DECORATIVE ELEMENT IN A HUGE WAREHOUSE
FLAT WHOSE EVERY SURFACE REQUIRED SCRAPING, SCRUBBING OR
SEALING BEFORE EVEN RUDIMENTARY BUILDING WORK COULD BEGIN

When Anne Bickford-Smith decided to give up designing textiles to become a painter, she knew she'd also have to part with her charming flat, since it was seriously lacking in both light and space. In fact, she was more than ready to move; quite apart from the requirements of her new life, she found the tiny dwelling slightly precious, and missed the sunny, open feeling of the homes she'd known as a child in South Africa. In the end, her search for suitable accommodation within her price range led her to investigate a type of conversion that, at the time – the early 70s – was almost unheard-of: a nineteenth-century warehouse. Anne chose her top floor home when it was still a single, completely derelict, space. It seemed to her that everything was covered in filth and paint, but she immediately knew it was what she wanted.

As soon as the paperwork was exchanged, she began to plan the layout of the flat with one of the building's developers, who was also an architect. Determined to keep most of the enormous area open, she sited the services (kitchen and bathrooms) in the middle; the adjoining bedrooms were given large doors that were meant to be left open to create appealing vistas and reveal uninterrupted space around the central island, which was designed with graceful arched openings, and walled in white. Above these enclosed rooms, there was enough height to carve out a separate studio with ample capacity for canvases and materials, plus abundant natural light from the huge skylights.

RIGHT: ANNE PLANNED THE CENTRAL STRUCTURE THAT HOUSES HER KITCHEN and bathroom as an island of white in a sea of brown brick, wood and tiles. Purposely left free of any ornament, this surfaces doubles, when necessary, as a screen on which holiday slides are projected. On the opposite wall is a series of Anne's pictures with strong African themes.

RIGHT: LIFTING furniture up to this top-floor space could have posed enormous problems: to help overcome them, Anne made full use of the efficient pulley system (on the wall, just beside the arched windows) that was installed to hoist the tea chests that were originally stored here.

LEFT: THE DINING TABLE was made from a boat's wooden hatch cover, treated with high-gloss acrylic resin. Suspended overhead is one of Tony's lamps, which can be lowered for intimate lighting during a meal, or raised high to give more general illumination. Seating is provided by Marcel Breuer's ubiquitous Cesca chairs.

Once the basic plan was implemented, Anne singlehandedly scrubbed her new domain throughout, then sanded and sealed bricks, scraped beams, and applied gallons of paint. The original wooden floors were in appalling condition, so they had to be replaced, then covered to cut down on noise. Because she wanted her kitchen in a different place from the one dictated by existing plumbing, an extra run of pipes had to be assimilated. To do this, and to provide a change of floor levels that would define separate spheres of activity, she raised the entrance and dining areas, creating what she calls 'the gallery'. This was covered in easy-to-clean, hardwearing quarry tiles, while the lower-level living room and bedrooms were fitted with natural coir matting.

Anne's natural affinity with wide, open spaces was a blessing when it came to furnishing and decoration, since only one or two pieces from her previous home were able to make the necessary transition in style, and money for additional items was initially very scarce indeed. Luckily, the windows aren't overlooked and they offer spectacular views, so very little treatment was required; the newly installed ones in the living and sleeping areas were hung with simple cane blinds, while the originals, which take the form of pretty gothic arches, were wisely left alone. The flat's only adornment was supplied by Anne's paintings, and a collection of figures by the American sculptor Herzel Emmanuel, an old friend.

Once she'd paid for a few basic items of furniture (including a fold-away ping-pong table that fulfils myriad functions), there was nothing left over for the bookshelves she desperately needed. An unlooked-for solution presented itself though when Tony Tooth, a new boyfriend, came to visit. An RAF flight instructor working in Dubai, he'd planned to stay only for the weekend, but before his cases were unpacked, he had a near-fatal heart attack – 'on my living room carpet!', as Anne describes it. He lost his job, and during his long convalescence became restless and bored, so she suggested he turn his hand to a little gentle carpentry. The shelves he made became, like Tony, a permanent fixture in the flat, and he so enjoyed the craftsmanship involved that he went on to design and make a range of domestic light fittings, thus establishing a career that has continued to support him ever since, as well as provide lighting for every room in the flat.

Despite the modern touches that Tony's lighting and much of the furniture provide, the flat is almost like a medieval hall; this effect is due not only to its arched windows, but also to the enormously high, vaulted ceilings, the exposed rafters, and the deep, antique-looking patina on the cast-iron pillars, a surface that Anne achieved only after rubbing in layer after layer of dark wax by hand. Located on one of the outside walls, the massive brick fireplace has a similarly early look, although Anne put this in herself, with the help of a local craftsman. To bolster the warmth it provides, and to add a more indeterminately aged feeling, she installed a solid fuel heater, endearingly named the 'Cosi Comfort' model (see the small illustration on page 118), which she infinitely preferred to all the more relentlessly twee designs on offer.

One of the qualities that Anne, and later Tony, most appreciated about her way of life was the pioneer spirit shared by the early occupants of the building, which had a faintly country-village atmosphere about it, with doors left open and countless cups of sugar borrowed. As warehouse living became more fashionable however, leases changed hands, the area became thoroughly gentrified, and the neighbourly feeling was lost. Suddenly, previously overlooked drawbacks (astronomical heating bills, tiring distances between rooms, and isolation from main commercial and cultural centres) began to assume greater importance, and Anne and Tony felt it was time to move on.

RIGHT: IN HER SUN-FILLED BEDROOM, ANNE ENJOYS WORKING AT A REGENCY zebra wood sofa table, sitting on a Georgian chair that she found in a junk shop. On the far wall, an artist friend's chilling depiction of the Kennedy assassination hangs above a Dutch inlay desk made in the eighteenth century.

Open Plans II

ENGINEERING WORKSHOP

IN A HOUSE WITH VIRTUALLY NO WINDOWS, THE DOMINANT
IMPRESSION IS OF SUNSHINE STREAMING THROUGH HUGE SKYLIGHTS
AND REFLECTING OFF ENDLESS EXPANSES OF WHITE WALL

By the time Anne Bickford-Smith and Tony Tooth decided to leave their warehouse, they had become permanently seduced by the process of taking on an unusual property and converting it to fulfil their own needs. They toyed for a while with the idea of a barn or a power station in the country, but the pull of friends and facilities in the city was too strong, and they settled on an industrial area that could hardly be less pastoral.

Their requirements were fairly rigid – they wanted not just a place to live and work, but somewhere with a good sized courtyard (a long-held dream of Anne's) plus adjoining premises for the interior design consultancy in which she had become a partner. Nonetheless, their estate agent found what they were looking for in the form of a disused light engineering workshop where industrial water pumps had been manufactured; when Anne and Tony went to view the property, the massive lathes and other pieces of heavy machinery used in this process were still very much in evidence. As soon as they saw it, they made an offer and put down the required deposit, sure enough of their future occupancy to make off with the beautiful old chair, also still in place, that had been filled by a succession of countless clerks labouring diligently at the company accounts. Then, having found such ideal premises, they had an anxious wait to find out whether they would be refused planning permission for residential use, but the fact that Anne's business was run from the same address meant this could be granted easily.

RIGHT: ON THE LANDING, AN EIGHTEENTH-CENTURY OAK CHEST OFFERS A dramatic contrast to the unrelentingly pale surfaces. The floor covering here is pure white carpet – guests are asked to remove their shoes. Above, venetian blinds not only throw attractive patterns of light, they also constitute an economical covering for such a daunting expanse of glass.

The couple were keen to retain as much of the form and character of the building as possible, so the external walls, although repaired, were largely unchanged. In order to squeeze in an upper storey, the roof was raised by several feet, but again the shape was kept, as was the huge, slightly incongruous, stable door, a reminder of the days when the building had housed horses for the local brewery. (They found further evidence of this earlier use when they pulled away the tongue-and-groove panelling in what had been the tea-making corner, to find piles of hay stuffed behind it.)

Inside, what Anne and Tony wanted more than anything was the feeling of space they'd enjoyed in their previous home – a large order considering this one was a fraction of its size. Several schemes were drawn up and discussed, but they settled fairly quickly on an almost open plan for the ground floor, with main activity areas being defined by the chimney breast and a series of low walls. Above this would be a gallery, with a corridor leading off it to give access to a small bedroom and bathroom.

When it came to implementing their plans however, their luck ran out. The first builder they employed, one that Anne had

ABOVE: THE ONLY ACCESS TO ANNE AND TONY'S Italianate courtyard (see page 124) is through a tiny door in this huge metal shutter. Inside, the impressive paving stones are actually ordinary concrete tiles dyed black.

LEFT: A HUGE EMPTY CANVAS AND AN AFRICAN hardwood easel identify the sunniest, loftiest end of the house as Anne's studio. The large, textured piece of wood is an old Spanish farm implement – it has inset stone chips to cut the stubble left in the fields after harvesting. The sculpture is by Herzel Emmanuel, while the light is one of Tony's.

RIGHT: OPEN SPACE, WHITE SURFACES, AND AN uninterrupted expanse of timber make the ground floor area seem much larger than it really is. On the chimney breast is one of Anne's bold expressionist pictures, and below this are the antique table and chair from her previous bedroom (see pages 122–3).

previously worked with on smaller projects, proved increasingly inefficient until, after three months, it became obvious that the task was beyond him, and they had to send him packing. His much more able foreman then took over, and worked satisfactorily until the time came for his annual holiday in Spain, from which he failed singularly to return, leaving the roof, the front elevation and the staircase unfinished. Of the workmen who were familiar with the job, this left only the plasterer, who seemed eminently capable of finishing it and would very probably have done so, had he not eloped to Scotland two weeks before the finishing date.

At this stage, Anne and Tony could do little but pick up the pieces and organize the remaining work themselves, which they duly did, despite the irritating inconvenience of a huge pile of equipment and materials left in the courtyard by their globe-trotting ex-foreman. For over a year they patiently lived and worked around this debris before they finally gave up hope and got rid of it, at which point the elusive traveller suddenly reappeared, only to sue them (unsuccessfully) for the return of his property.

The finished house, cool and stylish, betrays no sign of the drama and aggravation involved in its completion. All the walls are brilliant white, both to provide an appropriate background for the couple's possessions, and to make the best possible use of available illumination; since there are virtually no windows (apart from a tiny one in the bathroom), the sun that comes in through the huge skylights has to replace the visual interest normally provided by

RIGHT: EXTENDING from the seating area (below) to the courtyard beyond, the combined kitchen and dining room are bathed in sun from both the glass frontage and the skylight. In winter, two vertical, wall-mounted radiators provide plenty of warmth.

BELOW: ON THE OTHER side of the chimney breast from the rest of the ground floor is an off-centre fireplace; flanking it are two Deco chairs that Anne thinks were made for an ocean liner or a yacht – she snapped them up moments after they arrived in a local antiques warehouse. The open stairway framed in the background was designed especially for the house and constructed on site.

LEFT: WITH ITS INTRICATELY CARVED OAK DOORS
giving onto the light well that extends up from the
dining room, the tiny bedroom has a rustic, slightly
Mediterranean feeling; the simple country chair and
linen bedcover do nothing to dispel this illusion.
Through the window, at the end of the courtyard, is
the other side of the shutter that sets off Anne and
Tony's home from the surrounding industrial area.

outside views. To make this possible, Anne and Tony fitted huge white venetian blinds that sculpt the light into constantly changing forms. In the evening, the house is lit by means of recessed spots on dimmer switches, a system that, like all the sleek, linear freestanding fittings, was designed by Tony.

There are no fussy decorating details here: when handles and knobs are absolutely necessary, they are plain and white for a clean, uncluttered look. The pitch-pine floor is made up of unusual 30cm (12in) wide boards that came from an old wharf, via an architectural salvage company. Since no two walls in the building are parallel, or at precise right angles to each other, laying these was something of a nightmare, but now their rather idiosyncratic alignment is one of the many things about the house that inspire great affection in its occupants.

In fact, Anne and Tony are happy that the home they designed with such care is exactly what they wanted it to be; they love living at ground level, yet value highly the privacy afforded by their almost Italianate courtyard, which is overlooked only by the offices of Anne's business. Although none of the internal spaces is large, each fulfils its function efficiently and traffic moves smoothly from one to another. For them however, the great enchantment of the house lies in the fact that, despite having lived there for over two years, they can still be surprised by an unexpected vista or delighted by the intricate pattern of light in a forgotten corner.

RIGHT: RELIEVED ONLY BY STRIPS OF DARK-STAINED
timber, the bathroom's dazzling white scheme focuses
attention on the only window in the house, and the
almost surreal view it offers.

BARN LORE

STONE BARN

WHEN THE ARCHITECTURAL LUCKY BREAKS WERE BEING HANDED
OUT, THE OWNER OF ONE UNEMPLOYED STONE BARN WAS CLEARLY
AT THE FRONT OF THE QUEUE

From the moment Charles Edwards acquired his barn, until the day he moved in several years later, his relationship with it was characterized by an extraordinary amount of good fortune.

In fact, he bought it almost by accident. When he and his wife were looking for somewhere to live in the country, the local estate agent sent them details of a pair of late eighteenth-century stone cottages that had been knocked together to make a larger house. The description mentioned 'outbuildings', but only on their exploratory visit did they take any real notice of the neglected barn, mostly because of its potential as a storage depot for Charles's antiques business. Its 60cm (2ft) thick walls were sound, and the corrugated iron roof was functional, if unlovely, so all Charles would have to do was replace the earth floor with a brick one to keep damp away from his stock of furniture. The property suited them perfectly, and they lived there undisturbed until their divorce several years later, when the cottages were sold. He kept custody of the barn however, and immediately set out to turn it into a comfortable home, with plenty of room for visitors.

To make this plan work, he knew that an extension would have to be added, preferably one that joined on to the main building seamlessly. His first piece of luck involved spotting, in a local field near his son's school, two abandoned cottages made from exactly the kind of stone and brick he needed. As it turned out, the farmer who owned them was a governor of the school, and seemed willing

Right: THE SCHOOLHOUSE WINDOWS THAT CHARLES EDWARDS INSTALLED admit streaming sunlight that plays prettily off the facets of a Victorian glass lustre; in the middle of each window is a casement section that allows it to be opened. The floor is made from beautiful old bricks laid in a herringbone pattern, a job that Charles took on himself with the help of his builder.

to negotiate. There was much more material than Charles needed, but the farmer made him an offer he couldn't refuse; if the site was cleared, he could have the stone and the brick for free. Intending to share the booty with his builder, he closed the deal.

As far as Charles is concerned, the most important part of any house is its windows, and on the plans he had drawn up for the conversion, there were windows everywhere – twenty-one to be exact – so the house would be full of light. Unfortunately, the only suitable models he found lacked an opening mechanism, and he was afraid he might have to get these remade, but again, just in time, a local builder offered him a set of twenty-four lovely cast iron ones from a schoolhouse being demolished nearby. A friend reglazed each one in small panes, so that several of these could form an opening casement section in the middle. The most expensive part of the whole conversion was installing these windows, even though fitting bricks around them was considerably easier and cheaper than cutting the stone to fit. Needless to say, the bricks Charles reclaimed from the farmer's cottages were ideal for the job, and were also used as detailing on the extension.

With the windows taken care of, he turned his attention to the doors. The front door, which leads in through the extension, is a new one, 1.25m (4ft) wide to accommodate large items of furniture. He knew exactly what he wanted in terms of internal doors, and was horrified to learn that a friend of his had just sold eleven of them, perfectly matching his specification. Nothing daunted, he contacted the buyer, only to find that he was a dealer, and very willing to part with his purchase. The price they agreed was only 25 per cent more than the original, which Charles considered to be extremely fair. Although the doors were in excellent condition, with working locks, they lacked handles. Unbelievably, just at that moment, a stranger walked into Charles's shop wanting to unload a collection of brass door furniture extensive enough to fit every door in his house, and was asking almost nothing for it.

When it came to replacing the roof slates, fortune smiled on him again; he found exactly the right style and quantity – for a very reasonable price – at a demolition yard in the next county. When he gave them to his tiler, the man recognized them as a job lot he'd sold to the same yard only a few weeks earlier, for only a penny less per slate than Charles had paid.

Left: IN THE MAIN ROOM, THE SPIRAL STAIRCASE HAS A ROUND BRICK BASE THAT looks rather like a millstone; this similarity was intended by Charles as a reference to the stairs' origin. Behind them is a gallery that gives access to the three bedrooms used by Charles' children and guests.

ABOVE: A SUPERAN-
nuated serving table
provides display space
for a dried-flower
arrangement and two
table lamps made from
old tea canisters.

RIGHT: DISCOVERED IN
his mother's shed, the
old brass bed was given
a shiny new finish and
an intricately-worked
cream coverlet.

FAR RIGHT: ONE OF
Charles' favourite
furnishing items is the
huge dining table that,
later in the evening,
converts to
accommodate a game of
billiards. Hanging above
it are three masonic
banners, which also
came from his mother.

Charles knew exactly how the internal layout should be organized. The original barn was transformed into a huge, full-height
living room with a mezzanine level above it; the master bedroom
leads off one side of this, while three smaller ones lead off the other.
The extension houses the kitchen, plus two bathrooms, one of
which serves the master bedroom. From this side of the mezzanine,
a straight flight of wooden stairs leads down to the main level.
Charles found these – in excellent condition and exactly the right
size – in the garden shed. On the other side of the upper level, access
is by means of a pretty, wrought iron, spiral staircase that was being
discarded by some friends converting a local mill. This time, his
find did not seem purpose made: the stairs were a little bit short, so
he had to fill in the space with a circular step made from bricks.

Once the walls were replastered, Charles covered them with an
all-over coat of magnolia paint, an ideal foil for his eclectic
furniture collection. Like most antique dealers, he lives with a
combination of pieces that he can't bear to part with, and those that
he can't get rid of at any price. The curtain rails throughout are a
gift from his mother, who is also an antique dealer; plain brass-
plated steel, they are actually 1.35m (4ft 6in) stair rods. Hung from
these, the simple curtains pull completely clear of the glass.

Charles Edwards sometimes thinks a guardian angel must have
watched over every stage of his conversion. While no one could
doubt that he was very lucky indeed, he was also extremely
resourceful in his search for materials and furnishings, and quick to
recognize those that were exactly right for his house. In total, the
work he did took about a year, but at the end of it he had
transformed a building that had entered his life as an unnoticed
detail on an estate agent's blurb, into an ideal home.

AN ANGLICAN CONVERSION

CHURCH HALL

UNBOUNDED INITIATIVE AND EXCEPTIONAL INGENUITY MADE IT FEASIBLE FOR AN INNER-CITY HALL TO ACCOMMODATE TWO ADULTS, ONE CHILD AND THE FACILITIES FOR TWO VERY DIFFERENT OCCUPATIONS

During the process of finding, acquiring, and converting their stunning living space, the one thing film-maker John Bulmer and his wife Angela Conner needed most of all – more than luck, more than expertise, more even than money – was extraordinary and unending patience.

When John first set out from his previous house to look at properties, he only wanted a nearby studio for Angela, who is a sculptor. Exploring the neighbourhood one afternoon, he was intrigued by the local church hall; large, light and beautiful, it was clearly well on its way to dereliction, so he decided to call at the vicarage and enquire whether it was for sale. Receiving no reply to his knock, he turned to leave. Suddenly, an upstairs window opened and the vicar, clad in a white night-shirt and cap, demanded to know what he wanted. Bulmer's resulting enquiry about the building was met with a sharp 'no', and the window came down with a bang. Again, he turned away, and again the window flew up. 'Maybe later', shouted the bizarre figure, before disappearing for good. Undaunted, John and Angela returned another day to press their case, by now resigned to selling their house to raise the necessary cash, and living, as well as working, in the hall. Finally, after a long and frustrating year of negotiation, their offer was

RIGHT: EVEN THE FURNITURE IN JOHN BULMER'S CHURCH HALL HAS PASTORAL associations – the massive dining table was a reluctant gift from one of his relations, a de-frocked cleric who was relieved of his congregation and removed from the vicarage when he ran off with one of his parishioners. On a less dramatic level, note the unobtrusive skirting radiators.

RIGHT: CANTILEVERED OVER THE BUILDING'S
street-level entrance is a choir master's stall, one of the
many exquisite fittings John rescued from an
ecclesiastical demolition site; even the shelves are
made out of wood from the pine pews.

BELOW: THE CARVED OAK PANELS THAT SURROUND
the kitchen display a degree of skill and intricacy that
would be impossible to find on any modern
equivalent that was even remotely affordable.

accepted and contracts were exchanged. The church's Dickensian officials however, would give no idea when the sale could be completed, so it was agreed that the new owners should take possession anyway – a fortunate concession, since it eventually took an unbelievable six years for the paperwork to be untangled.

Once installed, they began the awesome task of renovation. Although they called in an architect to draw up the plans needed to meet local building regulations, they did every bit of the work themselves, with no professional help apart from an assortment of enthusiastic friends.

Since the main part of the building was completely open, they first had to install an upper floor – theirs has a steel and timber frame covered with chipboard, its level dictated by the base of the huge gothic windows. On this, they laid oversized black and white vinyl tiles that give the impression of an endless expanse of marble. Crisp white paint was then applied to the brick walls, while the massive wooden rafters were simply cleaned and polished.

To retain warmth, a vital consideration in a space this size, John and Angela inserted a thick layer of fibreglass in the gap between the roof and the vaulted ceiling, which follows the roof's original line. This insulation is obviously effective, since an ordinary

domestic boiler provides adequate heating in even the most freezing temperatures.

One of the room's striking features is the intricately carved oak panelling that encloses the small kitchen. This, along with all the shelves and much of the detailing, came from a church that was being torn down and replaced. Making good use of his winning ways with eccentric clerics, he offered the resident vicar a sum for the old fashioned fittings – pews, pulpit, screen, everything – that would barely cover a single luxury kitchen unit.

Near the kitchen, leading off the main area, are a bathroom and two small plain bedrooms, one of which also gives on to a high, sunny conservatory, an extensive project that was completed some time after the main conversion.

It seems likely now, though, that there will be no more building work; despite their extensive abilities and experience, John and Angela are not the type to make constant alterations, or to move frequently. Also, since they both work in this capacious building (on the ground floor), as well as live there, a replacement would be difficult to find. In fact, when asked whether there was any feature of their home that they wanted to change, or anything they'd do differently, John and Angela answered, 'No, nothing – this is ideal'.

Above: LIKE THE BOOK SHELVES, THOSE IN THE kitchen were made from pine pews. Next to the cooking area, through the huge arched windows, is John and Angela's plant-filled conservatory.

WATER
COLOURS
WAREHOUSE

A POTENTIALLY AWKWARD COMMERCIAL SPACE HAS BEEN GIVEN AN
INSPIRED DESIGN SCHEME THAT MAKES SUBTLE AND INVENTIVE USE OF
THE DRAMATIC EXPANSE OF WATER IT OVERLOOKS

The river Thames is much more than a part of the view from Rose
and Mark Flawn Thomas's warehouse flat; it's almost a part of the
flat itself. Since it flows right up to the building, and just a few feet
below the huge windows and the balcony, its movement, its
changing colours and its people have even come to play an
important role in the couple's everyday lives.

Rose originally bought the property by herself, just before she
became engaged to Mark, an investment manager. Like most
warehouse dwellers, she was after light and space in large quantities, and her work as a painter (she exhibits under her maiden name,
Rose Cecil) made these qualities even more vital. Although she had
always been attracted to water, the still rather bleak London
docklands were not her first choice as an area to live in; the scarcity
of suitable studio space however, combined with its exorbitant
cost, made her broaden her scope and investigate its potential. By
the time she came to look at this building, all the flats on the
fashionable upper floors had been snapped up; running at right
angles to the river, these had views overlooking the water, but at
one end only. She was amazed and delighted though, to find that a
long, narrow ground floor space, about 7×21m (23×70ft),
running right along the water with seven huge windows giving on
to it, was still available.

RIGHT: TAKEN FROM THE SEATING AREA, THIS VIEW IS OF THE MAIN ROOM'S
dining/kitchen end (detail above); the flat's open front door is just behind the
pillar on the left. The rectangular throw cushion, like most of the others, was
made from an old Turkish saddle bag, and the ornate mirror on the kitchen's
partition wall is on permanent loan (Rose hopes) from her family.

She made an offer on the spot, and was soon the owner of a completely empty shell – no walls, no plaster, no plumbing, nothing – a prospect both thrilling and terrifying. Despite her skills and experience with colour and form, she knew she'd need specialist help in planning and decorating such an unusual space, and in making it fulfil all the functions she had in mind for it: as living room, kitchen, dining room, bedroom and bathroom, plus artist's studio. At this stage, she asked four interior decorators to look at the flat and come up with a scheme; while three of them immediately waved pattern books around and talked brightly of swags and pelmets, the fourth, American designer George Powers, quietly sat her down and asked her to describe her way of life, her feelings about her home, and what she required from it. Recognizing the kind of approach she was happy with, she asked him to take on the job.

This early drawing-out process is an important one to Powers, who sees himself as an interpreter of his client's needs and tastes rather than a creator of his own schemes. As a result, his rooms feel very much as if they have evolved naturally around the lives of their occupants, with no hint of the often sterile look of many professionally decorated interiors.

The first thing he did was lower the floor of the flat by about 60cm (2ft), an inspired move that not only raised the ceiling to nearly 3.5m (11ft), a more suitable height for its extraordinary shape, but also brought its most important feature – the seven enormous windows (unencumbered by swag or pelmet) – up to the ideal sight level. Their dominance is illustrated particularly clearly when, once in a while, a huge destroyer steams by with the ship's full complement at attention – for a few heart-catching moments, the dramatic tableau blocks out everything else and seems to fill the room completely.

Both Rose and George felt instinctively that the flat should be left as one huge open area, with internal walls added only where they were absolutely necessary. Different areas of activity however, would be clearly defined by careful positioning of furniture. This 'articulating' of space is another thing Powers feels strongly about, since it's his belief that rooms must have some kind of psychological anchor in order to work successfully. For Rose, this was particularly important, since her family home is a great seventeenth-century estate (Hatfield House), where each room has its own very particular function.

When it came to choosing the flat's dominant colour, Rose's faith in her designer was sorely tested: the one he wanted – the subtle shade of an artist's canvas – was, in fact, cream, which she had always detested. To her eternal gratitude however, he talked her

LEFT: DIVIDING THE dining area from the rest of the room is a small ship's piano, which has one octave less than a standard model. At the far end is the couple's open-plan sleeping space (a far cry from the four-poster beds of Rose's childhood), while perched on a sailcloth sofa, waiting patiently for *their* bedtime, are a few of Rose's 34 teddy bears.

RIGHT: IN THE kitchen, specially cut glass shelves give an illusion of space; supported neatly with cable clips, they are easy to remove for cleaning. Separated from the dining area by a freestanding, ceiling-height island that houses large appliances (see illustration on page 143), the room has access from both ends, a common feature in Edwardian kitchens, and one that George Powers feels should be more widely adopted.

round, with results that could hardly be more successful. As well as making the space look much larger (ironically, despite the flat's large floor area, its extreme narrowness made small-space tactics necessary), the rich cream, a mix that includes minute amounts of ultramarine and burnt umber, provides a perfect background for pictures and furniture, and gives the whole place a warm, intimate feeling. The most glorious aspect of the paintwork however, is its finish – a shine so high that the rippling water outside is reflected on the walls and ceiling. To achieve the required depth, diluted gloss paint was brushed over a base coat of matt emulsion, a technique that is trickier than it sounds, as the decorators found out; their first attempt was rejected, and they had to do it all over again.

In terms of design style, all Rose stipulated was that the room should be of the twentieth century, but not identifiably from any part of it. This has been done by combining new, but classically proportioned, items with those that were passed on from her family, some of them, like the large ornate mirror, on semi-permanent loan. Eventually, she would like to be in a position to commission original pieces that will become the antiques of tomorrow. On the practical side, her main requirement was storage; she believes in providing approximately twice the amount that seems necessary, and this turned out to be about right. To this end, Powers has filled every corner and cranny with drawers and cupboards – either obvious or concealed.

Again to cope with space restrictions, clever use has been made of built-in fittings; running intermittently around the room, for example, is a low shelf cantilevered out from the wall, which, chameleon-like, can act as a storage/display surface, or, covered with cushions, provide extra seating. In the dining area, fitting perfectly into the frame of the window, is a large table, hinged across its width so part of it can be folded away into the recess when it's not required. The only problem with this design, complains Rose, is that its generous depth prevents dinner party guests from chatting over it comfortably, a serious drawback when shy strangers are trying to get acquainted.

Powers has given the flat a nautical theme by adding a variety of subtle touches like natural sisal matting, sailcloth-upholstered seating, bookcases supported by ship's rope, and a port-hole shaped mirror in the bathroom, flanked by silk-shaded Billy Baldwin lamps. Perhaps the wittiest of all is tucked away in one of the flat's two lavatories: the room is too tiny to accommodate a conventional basin, so an aluminium fish kettle has been plumbed in instead, with a hole drilled in the bottom for drainage.

Apart from a slight, wistful longing for a garden, Rose and Mark are completely happy in their riverside home, and talk feelingly of the lovely, peaceful atmosphere. Rose illustrates its potency by relating a delightful story of how, before she moved in, and when the builders were still on site, she brought a priest to bless the flat. Not surprisingly, the workmen were rather nonplussed by his evocation of the dwelling's spirit, shuffling their feet self-consciously and not knowing quite where to look. By the time he was finished, though, they had fallen under its spell completely – their heads were bowed and still, and they even murmured a reverent 'amen'.

ABOVE: THE BATHROOM'S NEATLY INSET BASIN IS actually a kitchen sink, chosen for its generous size and stainless steel finish, which coordinates with the chrome taps; the narrow grids on either side are heating vents. The tiled bath is completely open to the main room, while the grooming area is tucked behind one of two tiny enclosed lavatories. Even though the flat was originally intended for only one person, these were installed to comply with local planning regulations governing the number of such facilities necessary for the flat's large floor area.

FLOATING FLAIR
DUTCH BARGE

THE SKIPPER AND FULL-TIME INHABITANT OF A PARISIAN BARGE HAS HAD TO TEMPER HER ROMANTIC INCLINATIONS WITH A GREAT DEAL OF COMMON SENSE AND PRACTICALITY

The story of Jillie Faraday and her barge has all the elements of an unusually slushy novel – instant and powerful attraction, temporary happiness, then a sorrowful parting before the rapturous reconciliation at the end.

Built in Holland in 1894, the barge, called *De Waeckende Boey* ('The Enlightened Buoy' is as near as Jillie can come to a translation) originally transported grain across the Zuiderzee. It was converted for domestic use in 1942, but Jillie's first sight of it was in the early 1970s when she was looking for a home with her small son Ben and her husband, who had been posted to Paris as an industrial designer with the Canadian diplomatic service. They bought the vessel on sight and lived there very happily for several years, until he was sent back to Ottawa. The couple never managed to settle though: their roots had been put down in France, and even if they couldn't live on their beloved barge (whose new owners had in any case taken her to Toulouse), that is where they wanted to be. He gave up his job and they headed back, this time to Provence in the south of the country, where for seven years they owned and ran a successful trout farm.

At the end of this time their marriage broke down and Jillie, child in tow, headed back to Paris to pursue her career as a freelance production manager for advertising stills and films. For some time,

RIGHT: SITUATED DIRECTLY ABOVE THE MOTOR, THE BARGE'S DINING ROOM IS a comfortable 4 × 3m (just over 13 × 10 ft). Meals are prepared in the tiny galley beyond (which contains a refrigerator and a cooker with a full-sized oven) and eaten from a marble-topped bistro table. All Jillie's china, lace and flowery fabrics have been collected on flea-market forays.

they lived in an ordinary flat, but she had always kept in Christmas-card touch with the couple who bought the floating home she'd had to give up, largely because of her deep and lasting affection for it. One day, out of the blue, they contacted her – he was being transferred out of the country and they wanted to sell. What's more they were very keen that Jillie should buy the barge back since, even though they used her only as a weekend retreat, they were too fond of her to have any truck with developers or speculators. With a heavy heart, Jillie decided she would have to decline on the grounds that, by herself, she wouldn't be able to cope with the constant maintenance the craft needed to keep it sound and in working order. The sellers persisted however, and talked her into reserving judgement until she'd at least paid them – and it – a visit. When she stepped on board, she was alarmed to find a very different boat from the one she'd handed over; standing empty much of the time had allowed damp to penetrate the internal walls, which were running with condensation. To Jillie, it felt as if the forlorn cabins were weeping, pleading with her to take care of them again. She had no choice but to close the deal, comforting herself with the thought that if the move turned out to be a disastrous one, she could always find another buyer.

With Ben, she navigated her reclaimed home back to Paris, a six-week journey that passed happily and without incident. It was only later, when she had the barge overhauled, that she realized how lucky she'd been; among countless other defects, the wiring was dangerously antiquated, and the plumbing had to be replaced completely. At her wit's end, she would have given up if it hadn't been for the sudden appearance of a guardian angel in the unlikely form of an expatriate Irish builder called Joe, who had been recommended by friends. Desperately busy at the time, but unwilling to let her down, he ripped out all the dangerous wiring and replaced it with a single bare bulb in each cabin. 'I'll be back when I can', he assured her, and three months later, without warning, in he walked to refit the boat from stem to stern. As well as being absolutely sound, his work was done in such a way that, even without any specialist knowledge or skills, Jillie could keep all the systems ticking over.

Apart from removing a false wall that had been added since her previous occupation, she had only to redecorate before the barge was her ideal home again, and this she did making very few concessions to its nautical form or original purpose; around the lovely wooden fittings that date from the 1942 conversion, are curtains of velvet and lace, cushions of flowery chintz, jugs of flowers, Victorian pictures, and charming bits of flea-market china and glass that wouldn't look out of place in a country house.

Below: FOR JILLIE, LIVING ON A BOAT DOES NOT involve any lack of modern convenience; as well as its full-sized Victorian bath, basin and toilet, her bathroom manages to accommodate (at the other end), a built-in washing machine and tumble dryer. Covering one wall completely, a huge mantel mirror seems to double the room's size.

There's no doubt though, that Jillie Faraday would rather live on the Seine than in the grandest house in town or country. She enthuses lyrically about her spectacular views, about the overpowering feeling of calm and peace that comes from the water, and the exhilarating freedom she and Ben enjoy to sail away whenever they feel the need. But most of all she appreciates the romantic camaraderie the river people feel with each other, the solidarity they have in times of trouble, and the everyday sharing of problems and joys. With her inimitable pragmatism however, she is quick to point out that, should this idyll be shattered by a spate of noisy parties or next-door neighbours she doesn't like, she can always up anchor and move.

ABOVE: DOMINATED BY PILES OF LACE AND LINEN, Jillie's stippled bedroom enjoys the light from five portholes and a central skylight. On one side of her bed is an unobtrusive speaker, stippled to blend with the walls, while on the other, a white-painted cathedral heater holds a tumbling ivy.

A MONKS' HABITAT

CISTERCIAN ABBEY

THE MEMBERS OF A TWELFTH-CENTURY RELIGIOUS ORDER COULD
HARDLY HAVE GUESSED THAT THEIR MONASTERY WOULD STILL BE IN
USE OVER 800 YEARS LATER

We tend to think of domestic conversions as a uniquely twentieth-century phenomenon, and certainly the last decade has seen a dramatic increase in the colonization of warehouses, lofts, coach houses, barns and so forth. Some of the most popular candidates for this kind of architectural exploitation in our increasingly overcrowded and non-secular age are redundant chapels and churches, whose generous spaces and fine detailing make them highly sought after as homes.

In the mid-sixteenth century however, there was a similar glut of sacred buildings in England, but for a very different reason – the reformation. An important consequence of this spiritual clean sweep was the dissolution of the Catholic monasteries, whose money and land were appropriated by the Crown, and one of the finest of these was Forde Abbey, built in the middle of the twelfth century by a community of Cistercian monks.

During the Abbey's first 300 years, little new building work was done, although it was peaceful, learned and prosperous, its third abbot, Baldwin, becoming Archbishop of Canterbury, then dying on the crusades with Richard the Lionheart, who he had crowned. Later, in the sixteenth century, Thomas Chard, its last abbot and a man of wisdom, energy and imagination, devoted his 18-year sojourn to the building's repair and reconstruction, accomplishing

RIGHT: BUILT IN THE FIFTEENTH CENTURY, THE ORIGINAL MONK'S REFECTORY was turned into a library about a hundred years ago, and its gothic feeling reflects the fashion of that time. The carved chairs still have their Dutch tapestry covers, worked in about 1640, while the massive oak table was made on the estate in 1948. The globe is one of an eighteenth-century pair representing the celestial and terrestrial worlds.

ABOVE: LEFT UNFINISHED BY ABBOT CHARD, THE Great Hall was not roofed until the late sixteenth century, after the Reformation, and its oak ceiling dates from that period; the wall panelling was installed later, in the seventeenth century.

RIGHT: LEADING TO THE GREAT HALL, THE Cloister was also completed after Chard's day. Later, in the eighteenth century, the Gwyns replaced its original plain ceiling with this elaborate vault, whose design was the product of an earlier gothic revival.

the task, according to one visitor, 'with incredible splendour and magnificence'. His most obvious legacy is the great tower over the entrance door, on which he had carved 'Made in the year of our Lord 1528 by Thomas Chard, Abbot'. Unlike many in his position, Chard handed his monastery over to the king peacefully, in return for the vicarage of a local parish. Within the year, Forde had been leased out by the Crown to one Richard Pollard, the first in a long line of tenants over the next hundred years, during whose occupancies the great hall was roofed and enough general maintenance carried out on Chard's work for much of it to remain today.

The next great period in Forde's architectural history began in 1649 when Edmund Prideaux, Attorney-General to Oliver Cromwell, bought the Abbey and set about transforming it in the comfortable Italian 'palazzo' style then fashionable, for which its monastic layout was curiously well suited. He shortened the Great Hall, converted the monks' gallery in the centre into a saloon reached by a new grand staircase, and added state apartments over Chard's elegant cloister. All this entailed little structural alteration, but the formal rooms were lavishly panelled and plastered, and their external appearance was brought up to date with large mullioned windows of classical proportions. Perhaps Prideaux's most important contribution was the fabulous Mortlake tapestries in the saloon (woven specially for the room and installed by his son after his death), which portray scenes from the Acts of the Apostles painted by Raphael for the Sistine Chapel.

In 1702, Prideaux's granddaughter Margaret inherited the house with her husband Francis Gwyn, who became Secretary at War to Queen Anne, and their descendants lived at Forde until the middle of the nineteenth century, making several minor improvements such as redecorating the state rooms and remodelling the gardens and the south front portico. When the last Gwyn went abroad between 1815 and 1818, the Abbey was rented to the radical philosopher Jeremy Bentham, one of whose guests wrote that he had been surprised at Forde's 'cheerfulness, and still more by the magnificence of the house'. He spoke of a 'most striking and beautiful effect . . . the rooms are spacious and splendidly furnished and enriched with tapestry which is some of the best that I have ever seen'.

In 1846, the last Gwyn died, and the Abbey was sold with its contents, first to a merchant called Mr Miles, then to a Mrs Bertram Evans, who made some modest improvements and repairs. The estate eventually passed to Mrs Evans's niece and her husband, Freeman Roper. Like most such families, they prepared their eldest son to inherit the estate, but he was killed in the First World War and it therefore passed to the younger brother Geoffrey and his wife

RIGHT: CARVED BY THE PRIDEAUX OUT OF A MEDIEVAL gallery, the Saloon was given a stunningly intricate plaster ceiling and panelled walls. Later however, when Francis Gwyn was presented with a set of exquisite Mortlake tapestries by Queen Anne, he removed the wall panels to accommodate them. Among the finest in existence, these hangings (detail above) depict the Acts of the Apostles, and were woven from the Raphael Cartoons commissioned for the Sistine Chapel. Also of note are a seventeenth-century Dutch marquetry bureau (left) and an eighteenth-century French writing table (centre).

Diana, who kept it together during the difficult days of the Depression and the Second World War. Despite many hardships, Geoffrey managed to replant the woods and the gardens, and lay out an arboretum that contains a particularly fine collection of rare trees and shrubs. Another of his outstanding contributions was needlework, a traditional Roper family occupation: every evening of his adult life, he immersed himself in a piece of tapestry or crewel-work, and many of these still adorn the beds, cushions and chairs at Forde.

In 1975, Geoffrey's son Mark and his wife Lisa moved in with their three daughters. A survey done at that time revealed not only the need for reroofing, replumbing and rewiring, but the appalling condition of the ceiling beams: mostly located under flat, leaded, leaky roofs, they were being held together by the plaster